I0476351

# Economics:

# A Simple Introduction

*Also by K.H. Erickson*

## Simple Introductions

Accounting and Finance Formulas
Choice Theory
Corporate Finance Formulas
eBay
Econometrics
Economics
Financial Economics
Financial Risk Management
Game Theory
Game Theory for Business
Investment Appraisal
Marketing Management Concepts and Tools
Mathematical Formulas for Economics and Business
Microeconomics

# Economics:

# A Simple Introduction

## K.H. Erickson

# Contents

| | |
|---|---|
| Introduction | 6 |
| What is Economics? | 8 |
| Four-Dimensional Economics | 16 |
| Data Points | 22 |
| Trend Curves | 27 |
| Diminishing Marginal Utility | 34 |
| Best Fit Trend Lines | 41 |
| Diminishing Returns | 47 |
| One Outcome: The Equilibrium | 52 |
| Every Possible Outcome | 57 |
| The Time Factor | 64 |
| The Short Run: Shifts in Trends | 68 |
| The Long Run: Transformed Trends | 79 |
| Overview of Microeconomics | 84 |
| Overview of Macroeconomics | 90 |
| Econometrics and Value Estimates | 94 |

# Introduction

As the title suggests, this book is designed to help readers understand economics. While many textbooks may give the specific details for popular economic theory this isn't necessarily enough to explain the subject, as economics often seems to communicate in a different language and follow a learning process which can appear strange to those who are more used to other subjects. In order to address this problem this book faces some common issues that people may have with economics, explaining how the subject functions and why, presenting the most important economic principles, and addressing misconceptions throughout. Most importantly of all it shows readers how to think like an economist to get the most out of economics. In simple terms this book aims to explain the basic principles and methods which are the basis for each and every area of economics, to prepare readers for any and all future economic analysis.

The next two sections explains how economics may be seen as involving several different but related dimensions. These include a simple data point, trend curves and lines which combine data points, the equilibrium outcome where relevant trend lines cross, other possible outcomes when the equilibrium doesn't occur, short-run shifts in the outcome, and the long-run where data points can transform completely. Several sections then build on this idea and explore each of the dimensions in greater detail.

With basic economic theory explained the focus then moves to using and applying it. An overview is provided for both Microeconomics and Macroeconomics, to show how the two fields relate to each other, and to provide an indication of the major topic areas making up the fields and the role they play in Microeconomic theory and Macroeconomic theory as a whole. Finally, the role of Econometrics is explained as economic theory becomes economic practice, and example data estimates are presented before they are used to find economic relationships and calculate equilibrium values.

# What is Economics?

It's very easy to get confused when encountering economics for the first time. While other subjects introduce new facts and formulas, suggest new ways of looking at the world, or explain different skills and abilities to learn, economics often doesn't seem to offer any of these. And if the apparent failure of economics to offer any clear learning and understanding opportunities wasn't bad enough, the subject also seemingly wants you to 'unlearn' things which you already know, and to instead follow beliefs which often seem counterintuitive, illogical, and just plain wrong.

The confusion over economics usually originates from a misunderstanding over what it is, and it would be accurate to say that economics is less a specific subject and more a detailed method with which to understand other subjects. While other academic disciplines turn their focus to developing expertise in a certain field and ignore everything outside that field, economics examines the entire world and all that exists within it. But it's not possible to examine the whole world together at once, and therefore the process needs to be broken down into smaller and more manageable parts, which can be dealt with one at a time. Economics seeks to simplify every aspect of the world down until it can be described in just a sentence or two.

Economics deals with a complicated and diverse world using generalisations, and these are designed to capture the basic foundations of an idea. These generalisations can later be amended to allow a limitless number of branches to develop from their foundations, each of which can support a different scenario and allow new types of analysis to take place. And the analysis is designed to allow predictions and estimations to be made on what is likely to occur, how others are likely to act, and how people should act if they follow their best interests.

Generalisations are made possible using assumptions, which eliminate all the scenarios and examples which violate the generalisation being made. Sometimes the assumptions are made in good faith based on supportive evidence or a lack of information which challenges them, and at other times assumptions are made which are known in advance to be wrong. Following assumptions known to be false may feel like going against the entire concept of learning and understanding, and this is why many people struggle with and actively dislike economics. A more helpful way to look at assumptions may therefore be to see them as 'temporary restrictions'.

Some examples of generalisations and assumptions used in economics may explain the idea more clearly:

*Example 1*

**Generalisation:** 'As the price of a product increases, consumers' demand for it will decrease.'

**Assumptions:** Substitute products are available at a constant price; product is a normal good where consumers want more of it and not less.

This first generalisation is clearly accurate, and in the vast majority of cases in the real world increasing a product's price will lower consumer demand (i.e. their desire to buy the product) and the number of sales achieved. One exception may be if substitute products which haven't raised in price aren't available to switch to after the original product becomes more expensive. In this scenario consumers may have no alternative but to tolerate the higher price and sales may not fall. The other assumption is that the product is a normal good where more of it is always preferred to less, and only the price limits consumption. If this wasn't the case then a price increase may not reduce demand just as a price decrease may not increase demand. To use an extreme example, if the product was a service which offered 'to shoot you in the face with a shotgun', then raising the price from £10 to £10,000 won't reduce demand just as lowering the price from £10,000 to £10 won't increase it. The unwanted product is the factor limiting demand here, not the price.

The first generalisation here that a higher price tends to reduce demand seems obvious and too simplistic to offer any new learning opportunities. Readers may wonder why economics often focuses on statements such as these when they are self-apparent, but as will be explained this simplicity can be a building block to wider understanding. A different example and generalisation in an unrelated field can also be a building block in economics:

### *Example 2*

**Generalisation:** 'Government investment can solve any problem in a country's economy.'

**Assumptions:** Government has unlimited resources to invest.

This second generalisation feels counterintuitive, and surely government investment can't resolve every single problem in a country's economy, as economic problems remain visible in economies worldwide despite repeated and prolonged government intervention. The assumptions noted explain the specific circumstances when this generalisation may hold, and they reveal that it may only hold if a government has unlimited resources to invest. As no government in the world has unlimited resources the generalisation will therefore never hold as the assumptions can never be met.

It may seem pointless to make a generalisation which will never hold up in practice, and this is often seen in economics. But once again it serves as a building block for further analysis, as the second generalisation and its assumptions indirectly reveal that the reason governments can't resolve every economic problem may be because they have limited resources to invest in problem-solving. A final example shows another alternative type of generalisation which may be used in economics and the assumptions it is based upon:

## *Example 3*

**Generalisation:** 'An equilibrium outcome is stable and reliable, and it can change constantly and randomly.'
**Assumptions:** Consumers, producers or government can affect the outcome.

Of all the three examples and generalisations this one may be the one most likely to be problematic for readers. The generalisation here appears to be contradictory, and surely there is no way that something can be both stable and change constantly, or both reliable and change randomly. This is exactly the kind of economics statement which will baffle many and make people hate the subject, and it seems to be counterintuitive, illogical, and wrong. And unlike examples 1 and 2 the assumptions here don't seem to change the analysis, and only back up the generalisation by suggesting that if consumers, producers or government can have some impact on the outcome, as they almost certainly will be able to, they will create an outcome which is stable while changing constantly, and reliable while being random.

Those who don't believe or understand the third generalisation simply can't see the whole picture yet, and they are looking at the situation from a fixed point instead of the real world scenario which accounts for the role of time. For example, image a scenario where a restaurant chef is deciding how many meals to cook and supply to customers. If 2 people come in to the restaurant together and both demand a meal then the equilibrium number of meals for the chef to cook is 2. Only cooking a number of meals which matches the number of customers sees everyone happy to keep the outcome stable and reliable, and this stability is what defines an equilibrium outcome.

If the restaurant chef cooked fewer meals than the number of customers then customers would leave and the chef would be miss out on potential business and profits, and the chef would be expected to soon figure this out and therefore cook more meals. This ensures that the outcome where fewer meals are cooked than customers is only a temporary outcome and not stable and reliable, to prevent it from being an equilibrium. A similar principle applies to the case where the number of meals cooked is greater than the number of restaurant customers, and the chef would be wasting time, effort and money on cooking food which won't be eaten. The chef would be expected to figure this out soon enough and therefore reduce the number of meals cooked, to prevent the situation where there are more meals cooked than customers being a stable and reliable outcome, or an equilibrium. Only if the number of meals cooked matched the number of customers would there be a stable and reliable equilibrium which could last.

However, although a restaurant chef cooking 2 meals is the stable and reliable equilibrium if there are 2 customers, the number of customers in a restaurant will change constantly and randomly. And if more customers enter the premises so that there are 8 people in the restaurant, then 8 meals cooked by the chef will be the new stable and reliable equilibrium, and cooking fewer or more than 8 meals will only be a temporary and unstable result. But the equilibrium will change as customers enter or leave the restaurant, as the amount of people who seek a cooked meal changes. This shows how the generalisation in example 3 may hold, and how an equilibrium outcome may be both stable and changing, and both reliable and random.

Looking at the three examples above together, the first generalisation on price rises tending to reduce demand describes a trend line. A second generalisation on government investment resolving problems in an economy to the extent that resources are available contains all possible outcomes, and it basically describes a container. And the third generalisation on an equilibrium being stable but changing constantly incorporates the time dimension. The use of the words trend line, container, and time dimension may seem out of place here, but they are useful to show the multi-faceted nature of economics. It can be helpful to see economic analysis as a four-dimensional process, which begins with no dimensions and only a simple data point, and ends with a four-dimensional result:

0D (0 dimensions) = a data point;

1D (1 dimension) = a curve or line giving the trend of data points;

2D (2 dimensions) = lines are combined to give one possible outcome of many, one face or side of a 3D object;

3D (3 dimensions) = all possible outcomes are represented, within a 3D container object;

4D (4 dimensions) = a snapshot is replaced by an examination of what will occur over time, both in the short-run and the long-run.

Confusion over economics often stems from not knowing which of these possible dimensions is currently being used. The next section looks at each in turn and explains when each may apply.

# Four-Dimensional Economics

This section introduces the four basic dimensions of economic analysis. Each of the dimensions will be examined and illustrated in far greater depth in the sections that follow, but a brief overview is presented first:

### *A data point (0D)*

A data point uses a selected numerical value of a chosen factor to find the associated numerical value of another factor of interest. For example, it could involve the selection of a product and a specific product price to find the consumer demand at that price as revealed by the number of sales. Alternatively, a data point could represent an amount of government money invested in a sector of the economy and the associated level of sector returns. Another possibility is that the point represents a level of resource inputs used for company's production and the associated outputs and completed units which result.

### *A trend curve/line (1D)*

A trend curve or trend line is simply a curve or line drawn through a series of data points to represent the general trend. A trend curve/line can show a positive correlation between two different variables if it is upward sloping, where a change in one variable is linked with a move of the other in the same direction, or if it is downward sloping then it shows a negative correlation where a change in one variable is linked with a move of the other variable in the opposite direction. For example, a trend curve or line could show that the number of sales a product receives is negatively correlated to the product's price, and an increase in price is generally linked with a decrease in the number of sales. Or the trend line or curve could show that the amount of government money invested in a sector is positively correlated with the level of revenue for that sector, and an increase in the former is linked with an increase in the latter. Alternatively the trend line or curve may show that using a greater amount of inputs is linked with a greater amount of outputs, and that inputs and outputs are positively correlated.

Note that a trend curve or line only shows the correlation between two variables, and it does not prove causation. This has two important implications. First, it means that there may be individual exceptions to the positive or negative correlation the trend predicts, and for example an increase in price may not necessarily be linked with a decrease in the number of sales all the time, only the majority of the time. Second, it means that the relationship between two variables works in two directions and not only one as with causation. For example, not only will a change in a product's price be linked with a change in the number of that product's sales (as causation would imply), but a change in the number of sales will also be linked with a change in the product price.

A curve also shows if the trend between two variables remains constant, or if the relationship changes as the level of one of the variables increases. And this turns out to be one of the most important issues in all of economics, and puts limitations on what is possible and what isn't.

### *One possible outcome (2D)*

Once a trend curve or line has been found the next dimension involves combining it with another related trend curve or line, to turn one dimension into two. For example, if the first curve/line gave the relationship between a product's price and the number of sales (i.e. a product's demand), then the other curve/line required would be that showing the relationship between a product's price and the number of units produced (i.e. a product's supply), as demand can't be met without supply and supply is pointless without demand. And if the first curve gave the relationship between the level of resources a government invests in a sector and that sector's revenue (i.e. the investment's revenue), then the other curve/line required would be that giving the relationship between the level of government investment and the related costs (i.e. the investment's costs), as the importance of the level of revenue or costs depends upon the level of the other.

The point where the two related curves or lines cross or meet is usually the focus, and this gives the expected equilibrium outcome where the two different sides of the equation are balanced and equal. Where the curves/lines cross is the stable equilibrium outcome as it's the only point where neither side of those involved are motivated to push for change. For example, if the two curves/lines creating an equilibrium were a supply line and a demand line, then the equilibrium would be where the two lines cross, and where supply = demand. At every other point either supply is greater than demand, and a producer is unhappy and pushes for change, or demand is greater than supply, and a consumer is unhappy and pushes for change.

## *All possible outcomes (3D)*

While combining two related curves or lines gives the equilibrium outcome which would be expected to occur based on the incentives facing those involved, that doesn't mean that the equilibrium outcome will occur. If the consumers, producers, or governments involved actively try to force an outcome other than the equilibrium, and have the power to do so, then anything is possible and any outcome may occur. Therefore it's not enough to only note the equilibrium outcome where relevant trend lines cross and all possibilities must be taken into account, where any point on a trend line or curve is a possibility.

*The time dimension (4D)*

The final dimension is time, and this may be the one to cause the most confusion. Everything involves time, and therefore some readers may struggle to understand how time can be separated from the other dimensions just mentioned. However, there is an important difference in how time is considered which completely changes the analysis. If time is treat as fixed and unchanging, such as making predictions for next week, two weeks ahead, and three weeks ahead, and never changing these predictions as the weeks pass, then time is not really being properly considered. Instead the effects of changing circumstances over time must be included to properly account for time.

For example, if a business predicts that it will have made 10 total sales by next week, 20 total sales by two weeks ahead, and 30 total sales by three weeks ahead, but one week into the future it has made 52 total sales, then everything has changed. The equilibrium target would no longer be 20 total sales for the second week, and 30 for the third week, and those numbers would be impossible as they had already been succeeded after one week. Either new higher targets above 52 total sales would need to be set for future weeks, or at the very least the business should adjust targets for future weeks to 52 total sales, if they were happy with what had already been achieved and didn't require any more sales.

A time factor is usually divided into two separate fields: the short-run (SR) and the long-run (LR), and the short-run relates to changes which can happen suddenly, while the long-run relates to changes which take an extended period to arise. For example, in the short-run the relationship between a product's price and the quantity of units demanded by consumers (i.e. the number of sales) may remain constant, although external factors may cause price or quantity to fluctuate one way or another. However, in the long-run the entire relationship between the two variables can transform completely.

# Data Points

The use of data points is the first step in all economic analysis, and every data point is really a combination of two separate points which are associated with each other. For example, the data £1, £2, £4 is of little use in economics as it has no wider meaning, but to say £1 = $1.70, £2 = $3.40, £4 = $6.80 could be useful, and Great British Pound (GBP) to United States Dollar (USD) rates such as these are used in currency exchanges worldwide.

In many cases empirical evidence and historical data will be available to show accurate and 'true' data points, and economic decision making is often based on this empirical data. However, theoretical and imagined data points are also useful and can reveal the impact which different data point values have on economic analysis, as this book will show over the following chapters. For example, a product may have been sold at a price of £30 and generated 8 sales over a period:

Price = £30; Sales = 8

This data point can also be shown on a graph to provide a more accessible visual representation. While one single data point on a graph won't give much insight it is an essential first step to prepare for more detailed analysis. A scatter graph is usually used to plot data points, with the number of sales variable representing consumer demand on the horizontal axis (x axis), and the price variable on the vertical axis (y axis). The graph for this example is below, with dashed lines joining the example product price of £30 and number of sales of 8 to give a data point, represented by the small black circle.

# Product price and number of sales (demand)

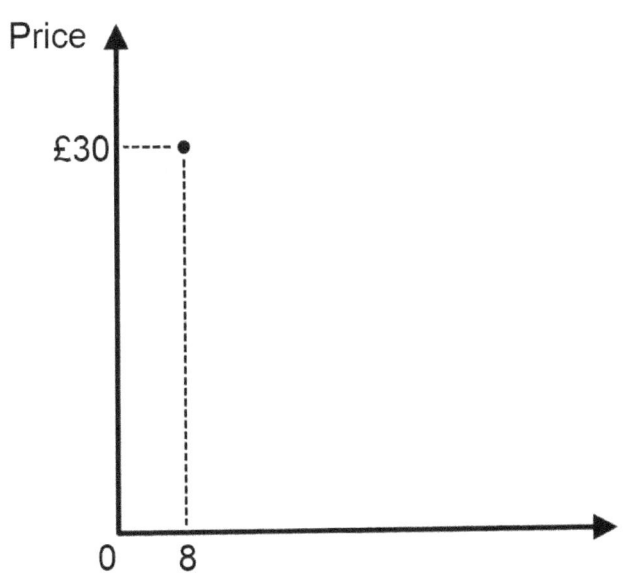

Number of sales (demand)

A move right along the horizontal axis in the direction of the right-facing arrow represents an increase in the number of sales, while a move left along the horizontal axis in the direction of the 0 number represents a decrease in the number of sales. A move up the vertical axis toward the up-facing arrow shows an increase in the product's price, and a move down the vertical axis toward the 0 number shows a decrease in the product's price.

With the first data point plotted on the scatter graph others can now be added, and perhaps instead of just one price for the product several different prices were each used for a period, as the product price was gradually reduced over set periods of time. This would allow more in depth analysis to take place, as the different prices could then be compared to the associated levels of sales to assess the impact of price changes on the number of sales. The following different prices may have been associated with the range of sales numbers shown:

1) Price = £30; Sales = 8
2) Price = £25; Sales = 15
3) Price = £20; Sales = 24
4) Price = £15; Sales = 35
5) Price = £10; Sales = 52

In this example a price of £30 was associated with 8 sales of the product (as already known); a price of £25 was linked with 15 product sales; a £20 price gave 24 sales; the £15 price was associated with 35 product sales; and finally with a price of £10 there were 52 sales. The following scatter graph diagram plots the 5 combinations of product price and product sales, and is drawn to proportional scale. As before the associated price levels and number of sales are linked with dashed lines, and where they meet gives the relevant data points of interest.

# Product prices and number of sales (demand)

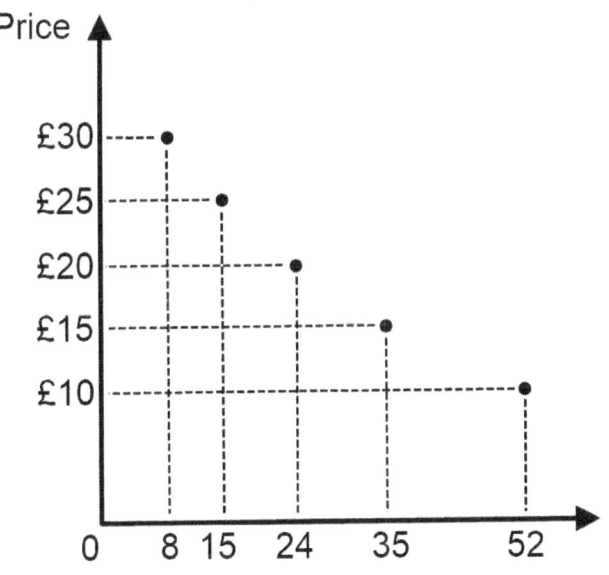

Number of sales (demand)

The purpose of a graph like this is to make economic analysis easier. Although it may be difficult to understand at first for those who aren't used to reading graphs, especially with all the dashed lines here, in time most people find it easier and preferable to see something in visual form in place of only reading about it. And once a person has understood scatter graphs they can be used to communicate key details far quicker than it takes to read a couple of paragraphs.

There is little more than can be done with only data points alone but the example here does suggest a pattern in the series of the data points. While the product price was lowered in constant steps of £5 the associated number of product sales followed a different trend. First of all the number of sales didn't decrease with prices but instead moved in the opposite direction and increased, and second the changes in the number of sales wasn't constant unlike the price changes which fell by £5 every time.

Despite the examples here not being based on real data and only using theoretical and imagined values the trend is very important. The trend visible here has been put into the data values deliberately to represent what is likely to occur in empirical data values in practice, and therefore it can be used as a representative of what could occur in the real world. The next section explains this idea further and looks at the pattern in the data in greater depth.

# Trend Curves

With a set of data points the next step is usually to search for trends, to find the deeper meaning that may exist within them. A trend in the price and number of sales example data was hinted at in the last section, and this analysis can be built upon using a trend curve.

## Demand curve for product prices and number of sales

The diagram plots the data points from the example in the last section and then adds a trend curve which simply joins the points one by one. This trend curve is known as a demand curve, and price and sales values and dashed lines from earlier have been removed to make it clearer. The demand curve is also an average revenue (AR) curve, as it shows the (average) price which the producer firm will receive as revenue, at various sales levels. The trend curve on the graph has the general shape of a downward-sloping curve, representing a negative correlation between the two variables. Here it shows a negative correlation between a product's price and number of sales, and as the price decreases (with a move down the curve) the number of sales tends to increase (the trend curve moves to the right).

However, although the trend curve simply joins all of the data points in this example that won't always be the case. When a larger number of data points are used than the 5 here they are likely to be more spread out, and joining the data points would only create a confusing and unclear zigzag mess, as the following diagram shows. As a result the data points should only be joined if this can be done using a trend curve that never changes direction. If the data points are spread out, as they almost certainly will be for large datasets, then a different method should be used. Instead of joining the points a trend curve should be drawn in one smooth move, in an attempt to pass through or get as close to as many different data points as possible.

# A confusing zigzag curve

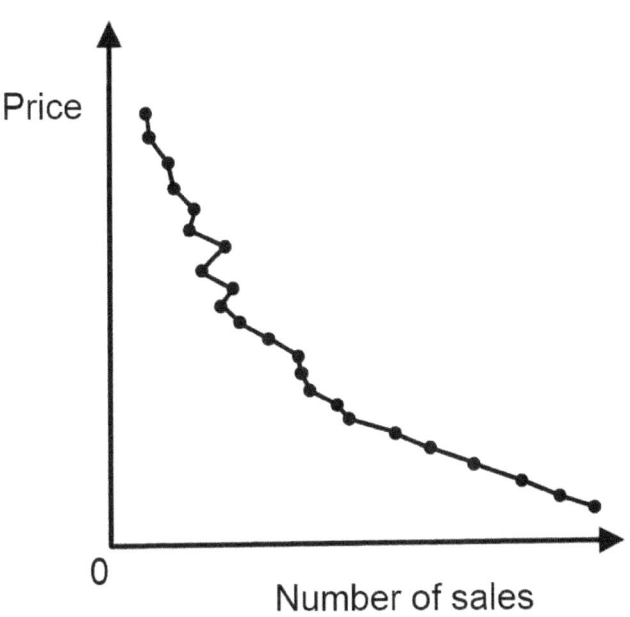

Price

0

Number of sales

The next diagram shows how a curve should be drawn if data points are spread out, and the same example with a large number of data points is used again but the confusing zigzag curve is replaced with a smooth trend curve. Although this demand curve is more curved than the original example demand curve with 5 data points the same general trend is visible as before, showing a negative correlation between product price and the number of sales. The visible presence of data points both above and below the trend curve in this graph supports the idea that the trend curve only shows correlation and not causation, as noted earlier. If the curve represented causation between price and number of sales every data point would sit on the trend curve, but there are visible exceptions to the trend. At times a price decrease isn't linked with a sales increase but a sales decrease (a small move down the graph sees some data points move left), and on other occasions a price decrease is linked with a larger sales increase than the trend line would predict (a small move down the graph sees a large move to the right from some data points).

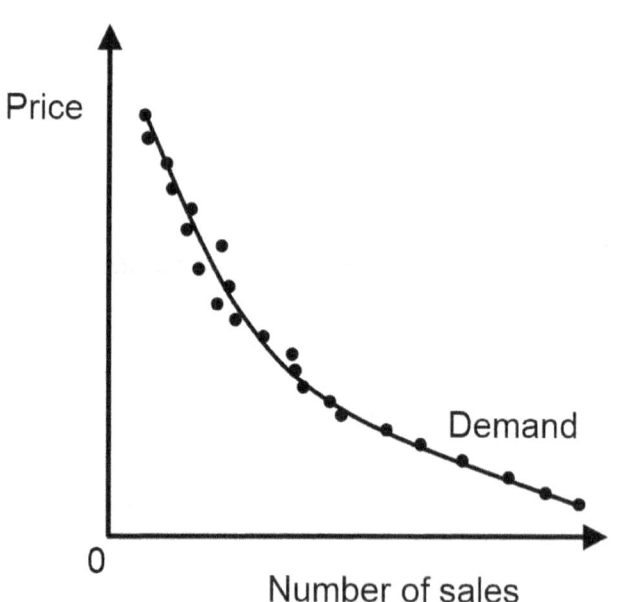

# Demand curve for a series of data points

If a data point deviates significantly from the general trend it is known as an outlier, but the presence of a few outliers isn't too important because the trend curve is only there to show general correlation. While a robust causation prediction may be possible in physical science it will almost certainly not be possible in the social science of economics, as it is based around human behaviour which can often be random or at least based on a myriad of complicated factors. Therefore a correlation prediction is usually the best that can be achieved. Note that while this last example containing many data points showed some data points which bucked the trend, the previous example containing only 5 data points did not. In order to avoid being fooled that an economics example shows causation and not only correlation it is therefore good practice to use a large number of data points in economic analysis.

Common sense would predict the general downward sloping shape of the diagram's curves, and a price decrease will usually increase demand and sales for any product. This is because of two factors; an income effect and a substitution effect. The income effect is where a price reduction for a product makes it more affordable, and the number of sales should increase as more consumers can buy the good with their incomes. The substitution effect is where a price fall has consumers see the product as better value than their current substitute product, and consumers make the switch to raise demand and sales.

It is also possible to use the curves on the graphs to note the effects of a price increase, and it simply involves looking at a curve from the bottom up. Doing this shows that a price increase (with a move up the curve) is linked with a decrease in the number of sales (the trend curve moves to the left). The cause of this trend is again income and substitution effects, but with a price increase they work in the opposite situation to that noted above for a price fall, and instead tend to reduce the consumer demand and the number of sales. The higher price has the income effect where fewer consumers can afford the product and this should reduce the number of sales, while the substitution effect would see consumers switch away from the product to better value alternatives to also lower sales.

Note that the word 'should' has been used for the description of the income effect for both price increases and price decreases. The substitution effect will always work as described, and with normal goods, including the example here, the income effect will work as described too. However with inferior goods the income effect works in the opposite direction, and a price increase is linked with a positive income effect (more sales as the good is less affordable), while a price decrease is linked with a negative income effect (less sales as the good is more affordable). If this 'reverse' income effect is large enough it can counteract the substitution effect completely, especially if the substitution effect is small as the product has few substitutes. The overall effect of a price rise could therefore be to surprisingly actually raise demand, and if this occurs with a product it is known as a 'Giffen' good.

To summarize, normal goods have greater demand (more sales) as incomes rise and lower demand (fewer sales) as incomes fall, with lower demand as prices rise and greater demand as prices fall. Inferior goods have lower demand as incomes rise and greater demand as incomes fall, and Giffen goods have greater demand as prices rise and lower demand as prices fall.

The characteristics of inferior and Giffen goods can appear to defy logic and an example can make things clearer. One example of an inferior good is gruel, which has been a staple food in many diets throughout history. If the cereal ingredients for gruel rose in price then simply consuming less of it would not be an option for many consumers as their diet depends on it, and more money would have to be spent to acquire the essential gruel staple. The increased gruel price and greater spending required to acquire it would use up more of a consumer's food expenditure, leaving little for the more expensive superior food items. With these superior food items now unaffordable the consumer could no longer have a diet consisting of gruel supplemented by more preferred food items, and would end up simply spending their remaining food expenditure on buying more cereal ingredients instead, to have a diet consisting only of gruel.

# Diminishing Marginal Utility

Looking at the relationship between a product's price and the number of sales reveals another trend beyond just the negative correlation between the variables. As the trend curve is curved there is what is known as 'diminishing marginal utility' in the data. To understand what this means and implies the three words need to be defined in turn. The demand curve itself is based on a utility curve, and it represents the need or want fulfilment of consumers (the motivation for their demand). A move along the demand curve in either direction represents a change in utility. A one unit change in utility is called marginal utility, referring to a change at the margin, the smallest possible change. And diminishing means something is decreasing in quantity. Diminishing marginal utility means a move down the demand curve sees a decreasing change (i.e. smaller rises) in consumer need and want fulfilment.

Diminishing marginal utility exists because earlier units of a product will meet most of a consumer's needs and wants to give large increases in utility, and later units have little more to offer. For example, the first few units of a food product may make a big difference to a consumer and meet their hunger needs and taste wants, but later units of the same product can't have the same impact as a consumer will be less hungry and will not be as stimulated by the same taste again. As earlier units of a product make a significant difference to a consumer they would tolerate price rises without significantly reducing their demand and sales, but as later units of a product have a reduced impact a consumer wouldn't tolerate price rises and even a small price rise will greatly reduce their demand and the number of sales. The idea is shown in the following diagram, which again uses the example of product price against the number of sales using a large number of data points.

## Diminishing marginal utility, smaller price rise, same sales fall

When the no. of sales is low (left of the graph) the demand curve is steeper and more vertical, and the product offers consumers large gains in utility. A large rise in price (price rise 1 in the diagram) will only result in a small fall in the number of sales (sales fall 1), as consumers are enthusiastic about the product and the utility increases associated with it. But when the number of sales is higher (right of the graph) the demand curve is flatter and more horizontal, and the product has a greatly reduced effect on consumers and results in limited changes in utility. A far smaller rise in price (price rise 2, far smaller in size than price rise 1) will lead to the same fall in the number of sales to consumers as before (sales fall 2 in the diagram, same size as sales fall 1), as consumers lack the enthusiasm for the product they once had.

This idea can be backed up with the 5 data point example, and the graph is shown with both demand curve and data points. At the left of the graph the total no. of sales is low, and an increase in price of £5 (from £25 to £30) is associated with a decrease in sales of 7 (from 15 to 8 sales). Dividing these numbers by 5 shows that a 1 unit increase in price (£5 / 5 = £1) is associated with a sales decrease of 1.4 sales (7 sales / 5 = 1.4 sales). At the right of the graph where the total no. of sales is higher, an increase in price of £5 (from £10 to £15) is linked with a decrease in sales of 17 (from 52 to 35 sales). Dividing these numbers by 5 shows that a £1 rise in price (£5 / 5 =

£1) gives a sales decrease of 3.4 sales (17 sales / 5 = 3.4 sales). The increased reduction in sales from the same £1 increase in price when sales are higher (= 3.4 sales), than when they are lower (= 1.4 sales), is evidence that a consumer gains less from the product with higher levels of consumption, to support diminishing marginal utility.

## Diminishing marginal utility, same price rise, greater sales fall

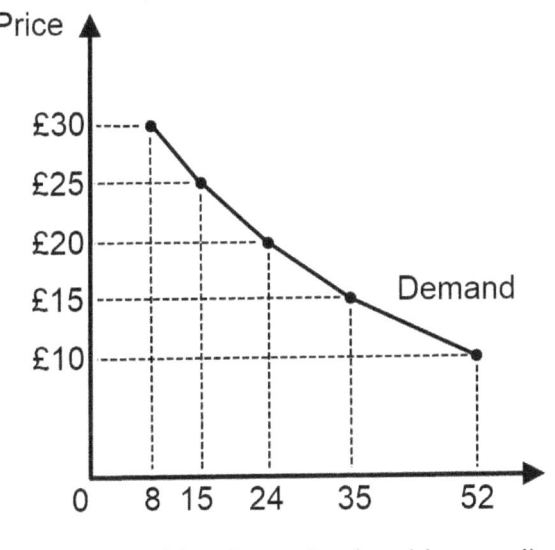

Number of sales (demand)

Many people who see this last graph will get confused, and insist that the marginal utility is actually increasing with a move down and along the curve to the right. They may look at the left of the curve where a £5 decrease in price (from £30 to £25) is only rewarded with 7 more sales (from 8 sales to 15 sales), but at the right of the curve a £5 decrease in price (from £15 to £10) is rewarded with 17 more sales, which appears to indicate greater utility.

Some readers may multiply the price level at a data point with the corresponding number of sales, to see the rise in sales revenue with a move down the curve, and may see this as strong evidence that marginal utility is actually rising with a move down the curve, and not decreasing as suggested. For example, at the first data point sales revenue would be £240 (£30*8 sales), and this increases with a move down the curve to £375 (£25*15), then £480 (£20*24), and £525 (£15*35). But the sales revenue would fall between the final two data points, from £525 (£15*35) to £520 (£10*52), and some readers may wrongly believe that this sole final change and fall in sales revenue is what is meant by diminishing marginal utility in the curve, and they may think that the rest of the trend is to be ignored.

Others who look at the graph may agree that marginal utility falls with a move down and along the curve to the right, but base this correct assertion on the wrong evidence using the effects of percentage changes in price. They may argue that at the left of the graph a price cut of only 1/6 (£5 from £30) results in sales which are almost doubled (from 8 to 15), but at the right of the graph a greater price cut of 1/3 (£5 from £15) results in only 1.5 times as many sales (from 35 to 52), for lower marginal utility. However, the ideas put forward in the last three paragraphs are all mistaken. They examine sales and sales revenue and take the point of view of the producer or supplier, but this is irrelevant here. A demand curve is not determined by producers or suppliers but by the consumers, and they don't benefit from a larger number of sales or greater sales revenue and won't base their demand decisions upon this.

Going back to the reasons for diminishing marginal utility, another reason why the change in utility (i.e. marginal utility) decreases, but remains positive, is because the relative change in the underlying factor decreases, but remains positive. For example, when the level of sales increases one unit from 1 sale to 2 sales the change is 100% ([(2-1) / 1] * 100% = 100%). But when the sales level increases one unit from 2 sales to 3 sales the change is only 50% ([(3-2) / 2] * 100% = 50%). And when the sales level increases one unit from 3 to 4 the relative change falls again to only 33.33% ([(4-3) / 3] * 100% = 33.33%). The positive but decreasing level of changes continues and as sales increase one unit from 4 to 5 the change is only 25% ([(5-4) / 4] * 100% = 25%). Diminishing marginal utility is following diminishing marginal sales in relative terms.

Some people may believe that the diminishing marginal utility linked with increased consumption levels suggests that consumption levels should be reduced, to try to secure a higher utility level. However, diminishing marginal utility doesn't mean that the overall utility level is falling, and only the increase in utility is falling. But although the impact of additional units of consumption may be less than earlier units they still offer something, and therefore a consumer will still have interest in them.

The diminishing marginal utility trend noted here tends to hold in all (normal) goods and for all consumption as the consumption level of a good rises. That includes both one product's sales relative to its price, and also one product's demand relative to the demand for another product when a consumer decides how many of each to buy and consume.

# Best Fit Trend Lines

Although the last two sections explained the relationship between a product's price and the number of sales (i.e. demand) as a curve, other sources often show this relationship as a straight line. Readers may wonder why some textbooks draw a demand curve and others seem to push the idea of a very different looking straight demand line, and often the same textbooks will use a demand curve in one chapter and then switch to a demand line in a later chapter. All of this may seem to be just another example of the contradictory and unreliable nature of economics.

The truth is that in practice the relationship between a product's price and the number of sales will almost certainly be a curve, due to the idea of diminishing marginal utility noted in the last section. However, a demand curve will usually only be shown in an economics textbook (including this one) to get across the idea of diminishing marginal utility, and after that a straight line will be used from then on to represent demand. The reason for this is that it's difficult to do much with a trend curve other than use it to show the general trend in the data points, but a straight trend line can be used as a building block for further economic analysis. A straight line can easily be calculated and given a numerical value, and this numerical value can then be used in various mathematical formulas to make predictions and assess the consequences of various courses of action. But this is not so easily done with a trend curve and a simplifying generalisation is therefore made to see trend curves as trend lines, although this will naturally add some inaccuracy to the results.

The following diagram shows how a demand line is formed when data points are spread out like a curve, using the example from the last section with 5 data points.

# Best fit trend line for 5 data points

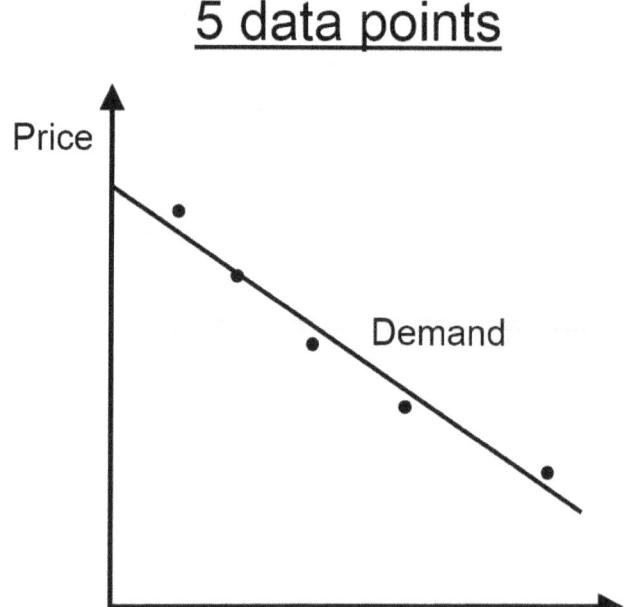

As the diagram suggests, the straight trend line for demand is a best fit line, and it is drawn to get as close as possible to as many data points as possible. This policy is exactly the same as with a trend curve, and the only difference with a trend line is that it must remain a straight line as it tries to fit the data points as best it can. The next diagram revisits the example seen earlier with a large number of data points, with the best fit line for demand here following the same principle.

# Best fit trend line for multiple data points

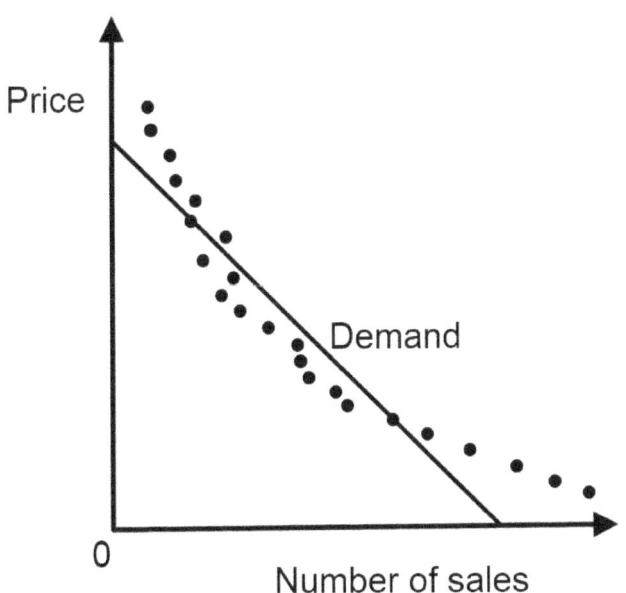

With a straight line used to represent a set of data points spread out like a curve, the focus can return to the issue of why this should be done in the first place when it will be less accurate than a trend curve. The answer is that two pieces of information can be found with a straight trend line, such as the demand line here, which may not be available with a trend curve, such as the demand curve shown earlier. The diagram below shows what these are.

# The intercept and slope for a demand line

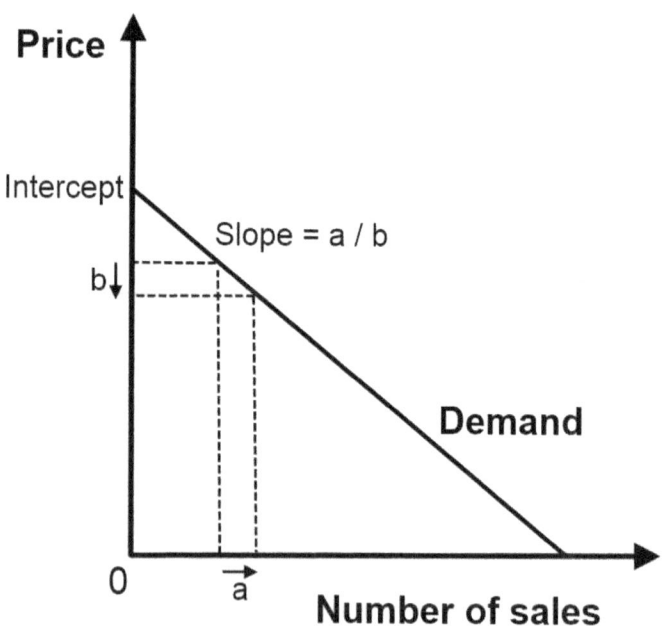

A straight line will have a constant slope, shown in the diagram as 'a' / 'b', where the slope equals the change in the number of sales (a here) divided by the change in price (b here). For example if a sales increase of 4 (a = +4) is correlated with a price decrease of 2 (b = -2) on the demand line, then the slope = a / b = 4/-2 = -2. And this slope would equal -2 at every point on the line, unlike a curve where the slope is different at every point which makes it difficult to make any firm conclusions about the slope.

A second feature of a straight line is its intercept, labelled in the diagram as a point on the vertical axis for the price variable. The intercept is the point where a trend line cuts the vertical axis, and although not every demand line seen in economics textbooks is extended all the way to the axis, if they are straight lines they can be extended to reveal the value of the intercept. This is one of the benefits of using a line in place of a curve, and a straight line will always have an intercept while it's possible that a curve may only ever move close to the axis but never actually cross it to provide an intercept.

Combining the slope and the intercept allows for one variable to be seen in terms of the other. For example, in this diagram price can be seen in terms of the number of sales, and price = price intercept + (slope * number of sales). As will be explained in depth later in this book, this formula or a variation of it using the intercept and slope for other variables is an essential part of economic analysis.

Note that the intercept is usually given for the variable on the vertical (y) axis, and the slope is found by dividing the value of a change on the horizontal (x) axis by the value of a change on the vertical (y) axis. The horizontal x axis usually relates to the independent variable (which can be changed directly to cause changes in the other variable), and the vertical y variable usually relates to the dependant variable (which can't be changed directly and which has values determined by changes in the other variable). As the diagrams so far have examined consumer demand and the demand curve the number of sales has been the independent variable, as consumers can only affect the number of sales and not the price.

# Diminishing Returns

Previous analysis has looked at consumers and demand for a product, measured as the number of sales at various prices. But this demand can't be met without the supply of those products. Supply will be determined by producers and is measured as the number of products supplied at various given product prices. Logic suggests there would be a positive correlation between the product price and the number of units supplied, and that a higher product price would encourage greater production and supply.

Many people get mixed up between supply and cost, believing the supply curve is either an average cost curve (like demand is an average revenue curve), or a marginal cost curve measuring the change in cost from producing one more unit. But a supply curve is not necessarily either, and although it may be related to marginal or average costs the relationship can change in different circumstances.

Example data points and a trend curve for supply are presented in the following diagram, using similar methods as introduced for demand earlier. The only difference is that demand plotted the number of sales of a product against its price, with consumers determining the number of sales, while supply plots the number of products produced or supplied against its price, with a firm determining the level of production and supply. As would be expected the curve slopes upwards, with a positive correlation between price and the number of units produced, and a greater product price motivates greater production. But as with demand earlier the supply curve only shows correlation and not causation, and not every data point sits on the trend curve for supply.

# Diminishing returns to supply, as the price required rises

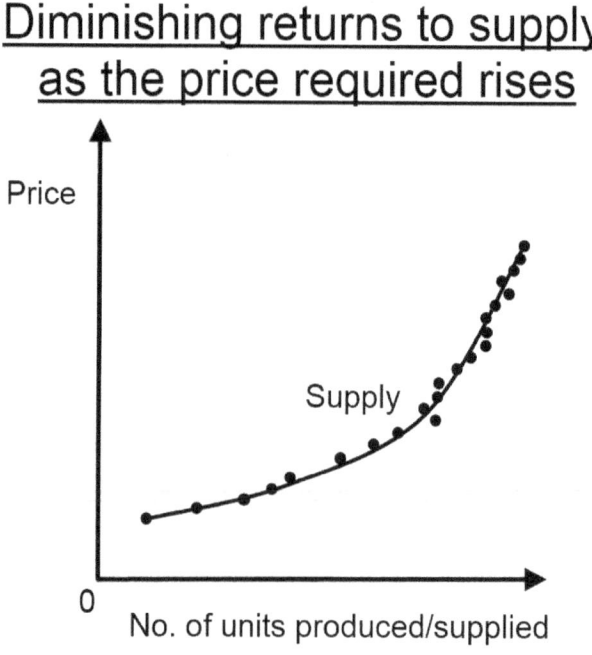

The curved supply curve shows a diminishing trend as the no. of units produced increases. At the left of the diagram with low production the supply curve is flatter, and at the right with higher production it is steeper. At low overall production levels a producer will increase production output in return for only a small product price increase (smaller rise up vertical price axis, more horizontal part of the curve), but at higher output levels a producer requires a larger price increase (greater rise up price axis, more vertical part of the curve). This need for ever greater increases in product price per additional unit of output is due to a firm becoming less efficient as production increases, and a higher product price is needed to cover this. Decreasing efficiency and productivity as production rises is known as diminishing returns.

While demand and the consumer side has been linked with diminishing marginal utility, supply and the producer side tends to be associated with diminishing returns. The two ideas follow the same principles, based around the idea that later units of a product offer less than earlier units as the earlier units have already met the important needs, and also due to decreasing relative changes in percentage terms. And just as with diminishing marginal utility earlier diminishing returns refers to declining increases in returns, and not losses in returns. Therefore a producer won't stop producing just because diminishing returns set in, as additional production still has something to offer.

There are two diagram specific issues which often cause confusion which are worth resolving at this point. First of all, it doesn't matter whether a curve slopes down (as demand) or up (as supply), or if it is curved in (no examples so far) or out (as both demand and supply), and all these scenarios can show a diminishing trend, whether for marginal utility or returns. Second, readers may have seen some supply related curves bend one way then another in the same diagram, clearly showing two different trends. In such a case the curve shows increasing returns (opposite of diminishing) at lower output levels, and then diminishing returns with higher output. But this doesn't change the analysis as every firm should push for higher production levels (beyond the increasing returns) in an attempt to get every last drop of output possible.

With demand the idea was a consumer's urgent needs are met with earlier units of a product (for higher marginal utility), the units which follow meet less urgent needs (diminishing marginal utility), and the units after those meet even less urgent needs (ever diminishing marginal utility). But with supply the idea is that earlier units can be produced most efficiently (for higher returns), additional units can only be produced less efficiently (diminishing returns), and units produced after those units can only be produced even less efficiently (ever diminishing returns). The logic behind additional units of output being produced ever less efficiently is that using more inputs, as greater output requires, has unwanted side effects.

The idea of diminishing returns can be summed up with the proverb 'too many cooks spoil the broth'. For example, a restaurant may employ one cook in its kitchen who can create one pot of broth at a time, but to make more pots of broth the restaurant will need to employ more cooks. However, employing ten cooks to work in the kitchen won't make ten pots of broth as they will get in each other's way, and they will make less than ten pots to show diminishing returns. Just like diminishing marginal utility with consumers, diminishing returns tends to hold for everything relating to producers and suppliers of any type of product or output. It shouldn't be an obstacle in the long-run however, as will be explained in the time section.

Once diminishing returns to supply is understood the supply curve can then be simplified as a straight supply line, just like demand was, to prepare for further analysis.

# A trend line for supply

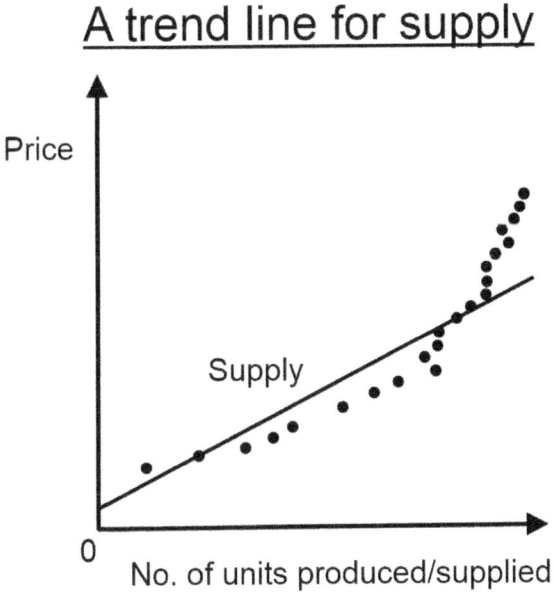

# One Outcome: The Equilibrium

Earlier sections created straight trend lines for demand and supply, and these can be combined in one diagram to represent both consumers (demand) and producing firms (supply) together. The demand diagram used the number of sales as the horizontal variable, while supply used the number of units produced, and to represent both in one diagram the horizontal variable simply becomes 'quantity'.

## Demand and supply together

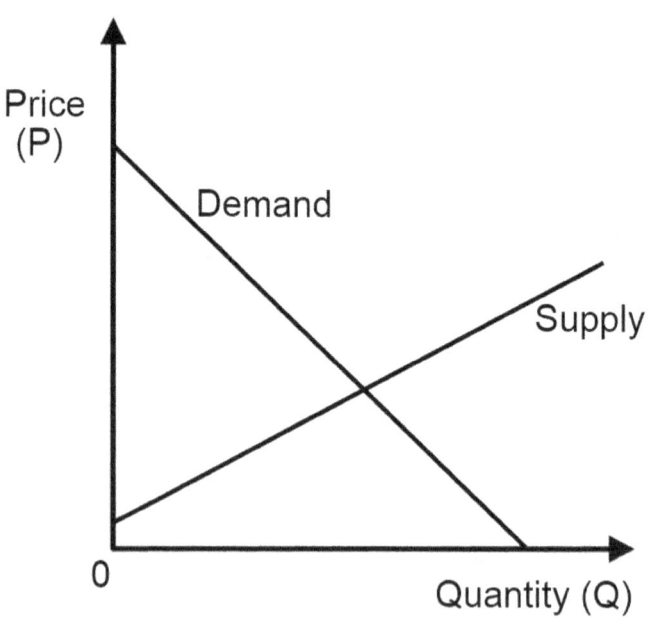

The downward sloping line represents demand, and shows a negative correlation between the product's price (P for short) and quantity (Q for short) of sales. The upward sloping line shows supply, and a positive correlation between the product price and output quantity.

There are five areas of interest in this diagram. The first is the point where the demand and supply lines cross. At this point, labelled as P* on the vertical price axis and Q* on the horizontal quantity axis in the next diagram, the demand price and supply price are the same (at the price level P*), and the demand quantity and supply quantity are also equal to each other (at the quantity level Q*).

The remaining four points of interest in the diagram are the various circumstances where either the demand and supply price or the demand and supply quantity are not equal to each other. With a price above P* the supply quantity exceeds the demand quantity (the supply line is further to the right than the demand line in the diagram), and with a price below P* the supply quantity is less than the demand quantity (the supply line is further left than the demand line in the diagram). And if there is a quantity greater and further right than Q* then the supply price exceeds the demand price (the supply line is higher than the demand line in the diagram), and if the quantity is lower and further left than Q* then the supply price is less than the demand price (the supply line is lower than the demand line in the diagram).

# Equilibrium price and quantity

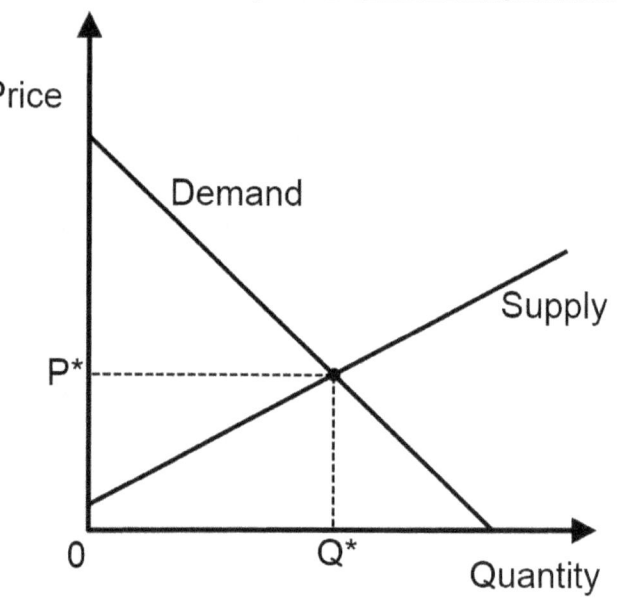

At price P* and quantity Q* producers and consumers agree on price and quantity, and are willing to make the trade and supply or buy the product respectively. This point is therefore the equilibrium where all interests are balanced and the outcome which is expected to occur. At every other point there is disequilibrium and interests are not balanced. Note that P* is just an abbreviated way to say 'equilibrium price' here, and Q* is just an abbreviated way to say 'equilibrium quantity', to save having to write these terms over and over and to save space in the diagram. There is no deeper meaning or mathematics to the term 'P*' or 'Q*' and their sole role is as an abbreviation. Any letter or symbol could be used to represent the equilibrium price and quantity levels, and additional methods will be presented when the diagrams have more than one equilibrium. The main reason a 'P$^e$' symbol wasn't used even though it may be more intuitive (with the 'P' representing price, and the 'e' representing the word equilibrium) is because this may confuse people, and may imply that a mathematical exponential (which also uses the 'e' symbol) may be involved, when it isn't.

If a product is sold at a price above P* then supply quantity exceeds demand quantity, for excess supply of the product. The only way a producer can then shift the excess unwanted units of supply is to raise the quantity of demand until it matches the supply quantity, which they could only do lowering the price they charge down to P*, with a cut price sale. They would then supply at the position on their supply line where price = P*, with supply quantity Q*.

If the quantity supplied exceeds Q* then the supply price exceeds the demand price, and products are too expensive for consumers and will go unsold. A supplier's products going unsold is the same situation as excess supply, and it can only be resolved in the same way with the supplier reducing the price down to P* in a sale, which is linked with supply quantity Q* on the supply line.

In the alternative situation where the product's price is lower than P* supply quantity is lower than demand quantity, and there is excess demand for the product and consumers go unsatisfied. Consumers can only get what they want if they raise the quantity of supply until it meets the quantity demanded, and only the incentive of earning more money per sale will motivate a producer to raise their supply quantity, and therefore consumers must raise the price they pay to P*, which sees them on a position on their demand line where demand quantity is Q*.

If the quantity supplied is less than Q* then the demand price is greater than the supply price, and consumers are willing to pay a price higher than the supplier requires. This is the same situation as excess demand and consumers are willing and able to spend more money on the product, but there are no more of the products to spend it on. The only solution to this is again for consumers to raise the price they pay to P*, to push up the supplier quantity, and this price is again linked with quantity Q* on the demand line.

Every point on the diagram should lead back to the situation where demand = supply, and where the price is at level P* and the quantity produced/bought is at level Q*, making this point the stable equilibrium where neither side is pushing for change and changing the result. However, the key word here is should, and although this is the natural equilibrium that doesn't mean that this will definitely occur. It is only one of many possible outcomes which could come to pass, as the next section explains.

# Every Possible Outcome

The equilibrium outcome noted in the last section, where demand = supply, is where the needs or wants of both consumers and producers are balanced, and it is the outcome which should naturally occur due to the incentives facing consumers and producers. But while this may transpire in theory it might not hold up in practice, as it depends on an efficient free market system where consumers and producers have equal power and influence, and this may not exist in many areas of an economy.

## _Government blocking the equilibrium outcome_

Many countries set a minimum wage for workers, and it is illegal for employers to set a wage price lower than that level. In the workforce the employer is the consumer, of hours of labour, and the worker employees are the producers, of those hours of labour. A minimum wage therefore sees the government intervene to block the natural equilibrium workers and employers would naturally reach, by preventing producers of labour (workers) from being able to lower their prices to P*. The following diagram gives the idea, recreating the last diagram and adding a price set at minimum wage (Pmw).

# Result of high minimum wage

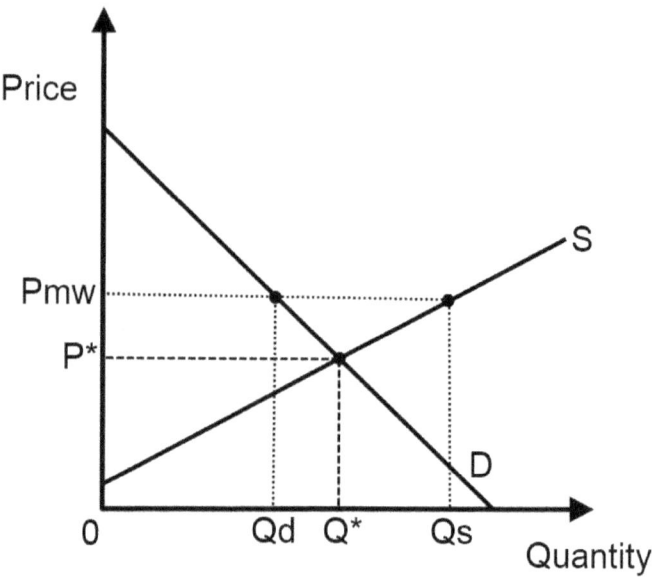

The diagram is simply the last one, with a few more dotted lines and letters added. Supply and demand are now denoted as only S and D respectively, and when more information is added to a diagram it's common to use letter abbreviations in place of full words to save space. The minimum wage price (Pmw) the government sets is above the equilibrium price of P*, and it results in a quantity demanded (on the demand line) of Qd in the diagram and a quantity supplied (on the supply line) of Qs. Qs is further along the horizontal axis for quantity than Qd, and therefore the quantity of labour hours supplied from workers exceeds the quantity of labour hours demanded by employers. This results in either worker unemployment or part-time work only, as workers are left unable to lower the price they charge for their labour.

A minimum wage may be set at any level above the market clearing rate (where demand = supply) of $P^*$, but it will never be set at the equilibrium price as this outcome would occur naturally without a fixed price and the minimum wage wouldn't be needed. A minimum wage therefore opens up the possibility of any number of outcomes where the price and quantity (of the product or service) supplied are above the equilibrium levels.

While government intervention may stop producers of a product from lowering prices to the equilibrium price, government can also often prevent consumers from raising the prices they pay to this equilibrium. Any government institution which rations the government's resources or opportunities based on the receiver's identifying group is essentially preventing those who would pay more for the product from being able to do so. For example, government resources (which are products) or opportunities (which are services) may be allocated only to young people, or elderly people, or women and girls, or those from certain ethnic groups, or those with low income levels, yet people who don't meet these criteria may be willing to pay a higher price for the resources or opportunities. And someone who meets the government criteria may actually be willing and able to pay a higher price themselves, yet state preference means they don't have to and therefore won't. Government support may therefore open up the possibility of any number of non-equilibrium outcomes, where the price and quantity supplied of a product are lower than the natural equilibrium. Supply restrictions by the government (e.g. import quotas on foreign products) which restrict the quantity supplied of a product or service to a point below level Q* would have exactly the same effect.

## *Government facilitating the equilibrium outcome*

The last two examples may have appeared to be critical of government, and lay the blame for any non-equilibrium and unbalanced outcome in their direction. However, in many cases there may be a need for government intervention, and without it the producers or consumers of a product may destroy the equilibrium all by themselves. One example of producers potentially setting a price above the equilibrium is with a trade union which represents workers and demands excessive wage increases, while an example of consumers setting a price below the equilibrium is with those who dump their harmful waste materials into the natural environment without paying to make up for the damage it will cause. In both cases a government has unique power to bring about a superior equilibrium outcome where all parties needs are balanced.

A powerful trade union organized by determined workers (producers of labour hours) may demand a higher working wage than the natural equilibrium, and stubbornly ignore all suggestions to lower their demands, willing to go without work to make their point. In this scenario a government could resolve the non-equilibrium by using state power to clamp down hard on the trade union, and to force them to accept the equilibrium price. Alternatively government may get the trade union to comply willingly, and offer a subsidy to workers (producers of labour) so they receive the price they want (government subsidy + equilibrium price $P^*$ = wage price union demands). Costs of a government subsidy would be forced on taxpayers, while consumers of workers' labour (employers, including the government) will still only pay price $P^*$ to ensure the natural equilibrium price and quantity of supply occurs. There would be limits to this subsidy however, and as noted at the start of this book even if state investment can resolve every problem the state still has limited resources to invest, based on what they can get from taxpayers.

The problem of 'free-riding' of natural environmental resources is one of the main motivators for government intervention into society. Without government intervention some people will dump their household waste, toxic waste, or oil into rural areas or the sea, using them as their personal dumping ground despite not having property rights over these areas, and not paying for their damage. In this scenario consumers and their demand will refer to the polluters (who are consuming the natural environment), and producers and their supply will refer to the relevant government (which acts as protector for their country's environment and nearby sea, to ensure the supply of natural resources doesn't decline and isn't destroyed).

A visual representation of free-riders not paying for their pollution is shown in the next diagram where a free-riding price, Pfr, shows what polluters would naturally pay, which is zero. This level of price is linked with a consumer (polluter) demand quantity of Qd, by looking directly along the horizontal axis until reaching the demand (D) line. And this demand quantity is far above the producer quantity supplied which is zero at Qs, and no point on the supply line is available with the free-rider price (Pfr) of zero. In simple terms there is excess demand for the environment's natural resources, and people will naturally use them up unless stopped.

The only way to resolve the free-rider problem is by forcing the consumers (polluters) to pay the equilibrium price, P*, to compensate for their damage. And this will ensure the polluters only demand a smaller quantity of the environment which corresponds to this price, equilibrium quantity Q* where demand (D) equals supply (S) and all needs are balanced. A polluter tax ('green tax') is the typical method used to achieve this goal, and this would need to be set at a level to ensure that Pfr + tax = P*.

# Free-riding effects

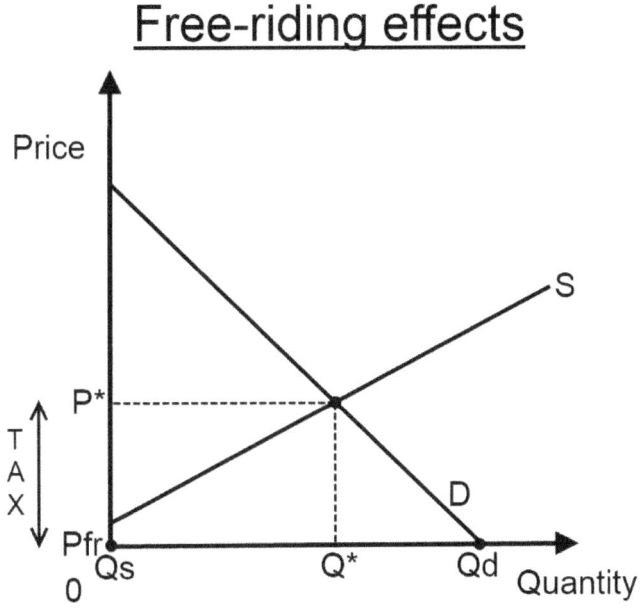

However, despite the potential problems in reaching the equilibrium noted in this section, either caused by government or potentially resolved by them, the equilibrium outcome is still the most important focus in economics. It may only be one outcome of many which could occur but it is the one and only outcome where all interests are balanced and where the result is stable. Therefore it is both the outcome most likely to occur on average and the one which policy-makers will target if they are focused on efficiency.

# The Time Factor

Despite the logical arguments put forward up to this point many readers will still have their doubts about economics, and while everything which has been explained may be plausible it can still feel counterintuitive and wrong. In simple terms the main problem which many people have with economics is that they just don't trust it. It's all well and good to be told that a certain outcome will occur, or that people will act a certain way, but when you've seen the exact opposite happen in real life or know that you yourself wouldn't act that way then it's hard to believe it.

The cause of a lack of trust in economics is almost certainly due to the reader getting confused over the role of time in economics. Time is often treat as a separate influence in economics to allow both static (a movement between points in time where needs and preferences remain fixed) and dynamic (flowing time where needs and preferences can shift) analysis to be conducted separately, to note the different results. And not knowing which of the two methods, static or dynamic, is being used can naturally cause confusion.

For example, readers may insist that they wouldn't behave as the consumers have been depicted as behaving in this book, who demand and want to buy more and more of a product as the price declines, with only limited supply restricted them. They may picture themselves as only demanding and buying the amount of products they need and no more than that, no matter how low the product price may then decline. Student readers may even be able to back this up with an example. They may point out that they've bought several economics textbook products at full price one after the other, and didn't require a price decrease to motivate their additional sales. Or alternatively they may have only bought one economics textbook, and insist they didn't want or buy any more even though many other textbook products were available later at a huge discount. Furthermore, readers may doubt the idea of an equilibrium price for a product, as they've seen the same products at different prices at various different sources.

However, readers' experiences are likely to be based on a flowing time (dynamic) standpoint where their needs and desires at every moment are recorded, and both their original need for a product and then their shifted needs after acquiring it are represented. The analysis up to this point has been solely focused upon fixed points in time (static) where a consumer's needs and preferences have been fixed, and represented by a certain amount of quantity demanded at one price and a higher quantity demanded at a lower price, but never acknowledging that these needs and preferences may completely change over time as their needs are satisfied.

A static analysis might predict that a student would buy one economics textbook at one price, and then (with some of their education needs already met by the first textbook) buy another solely because it was in a sale with 50% off the normal price. Then that same student may buy a third textbook which had 20% of the normal price, as they were already in the habit of buying textbooks, and they didn't need another 50% discount to motivate the sale as they'd already got a great deal with 50% off the last book. This all follows the idea of diminishing marginal utility explained earlier, and a curved demand function.

However, a dynamic analysis may acknowledge the possibility that the first economics textbook was fantastic and flawless in explaining everything about the subject, and that no further textbooks were needed at all even if they were free. Dynamic analysis may also acknowledge the possibility that the first textbook was terrible and useless, and that a second economics textbook had to be bought, even though it was at its full undiscounted price, as the first book had not met any of the consumer's needs. The difference is that dynamic analysis allows for unpredicted shifts in needs, while static analysis expects everything to be predictable.

Adding dynamic economic analysis to the discussion not only makes more intuitive sense to readers, but it also can explain why certain predicted outcomes may not come to pass. For example, there has been much talk of an equilibrium outcome for a product where consumer and producer goals are met, and where supply = demand. However, in the real world there is of course no such thing as only one equilibrium price for a product, and at any time one product will have a range of different prices for different areas. A product may have one price in one branch of a chain store, while the exact same product has a completely different price in a different branch of the same brand of chain store. The producer/supplier would be the same in both cases (the chain store) which should keep the supply line the same for both, and presumably consumers who go to one branch of the store would also go to another which should keep the demand line the same for both chain stores too. With demand and supply lines still the same for both chain stores a static form of analysis can't explain why they might have different prices, but a dynamic analysis can using the idea of shifts in demand or supply which cause a shift in the price. The next section examines this idea of shifts in the demand and supply trends represented by demand and supply lines in more depth.

# The Short Run: Shifts in Trends

Dynamic economic analysis allows for free flowing time where things can change at any moment, in place of static analysis where conditions are assumed to remain constant. Dynamic analysis can be separated into two parts: the short-run with changes or shifts which can occur suddenly, and the long-run with changes in trends which take a long period of time to come about. This section looks at the short-run time factor, which uses the foundations provided by static analysis trend lines and equilibrium predictions, but adds the possibility for shifts in demand or supply one way or another. These shifts may be long-lasting or may disappear very quickly, and what defines the short-run time factor is not that the duration of the effects but how quickly they materialize in the first place, as in the short-run no-one can know how long effects will last.

## *Increase in demand*

The following diagram provides an example of what can happen in a short period of time, as the example with equilibrium of price P* and quantity Q* is reproduced but another line has been added to the diagram, D1. D1 is a new dashed demand line that may replace demand line D in certain short-run circumstances, and the 1 in D1 could stand for 1 hour ahead, 1 day ahead, or 1 week ahead. Line D1 has the same slope as line D, but the intercept has increased to see the demand line shift right from D to parallel D1. This shift sees the relevant demand line (now D1) cut supply at a new point for a new equilibrium, with higher equilibrium price P1 and higher equilibrium quantity sold Q1. Producers or suppliers gain from this and will therefore hope for increases in demand.

# Result of increase in demand

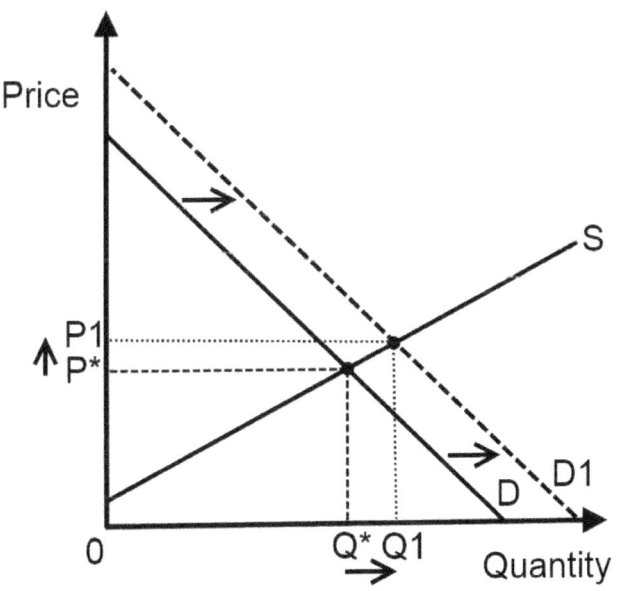

There are any number of possible causes for a sudden rightwards parallel shift in the demand line like this. Consumers may have suddenly received an increase in income which gives them more money to spend on the product to push up demand at every possible product price; or the price of substitute products may have increased to see consumers turn away from those goods and purchase a greater quantity of the product here instead. Alternatively, the producer of the product here may have ran a good advertising campaign which impressed consumers, who increased their demand and number of sales of the advertised product accordingly. All of these three possible scenarios are examples of situations where a sudden shift in the demand line could be long-lasting, and could cause the demand line to move from D to D1 permanently.

There is also an example of a demand shift which may temporary, and this relates back to the idea of two chain stores with different prices from the last section. One of the chain stores may be based where there are competitors nearby selling substitute products, such as in a shopping centre, and this could see demand shared between the competitors. This would give the chain store's product the level of demand shown by the original demand line (D), for an equilibrium with price P* and quantity sold Q*. But the other chain store may have no competitors nearby, for example if it was based at an airport, and consumers who pass won't have easy access to substitute products and must give all of their demand for the product to that store. The second store will have higher demand at every price and the new demand line (D1) may represent this higher demand, for a new equilibrium with a higher price such as P1 and a higher quantity sold of the chain store's products such as at Q1. As consumers move from the shopping centre to the airport their demand would shift from D to D1, but after leaving the airport it would shift back to D.

The previous diagram and rightward shift in demand can also be used to explain the example in the last section with students buying economics textbooks. In normal circumstances with a textbook of a relatively good quality a student may stay on the original demand curve, D, and only buy additional textbooks if the price falls (represented by the downward sloping demand line, D). But if the first economics textbook purchased was truly terrible, and it not only failed to offer any insight into the subject but actually reduced the student's level of understanding, then it's possible the student may become desperate for another economics textbook to make up for the problems caused by the first. This desperation could feasibly cause a parallel shift in the demand curve rightwards from D to D1, with an increased quantity of products demanded at every product price, and therefore the student would be willing to pay the same (full) price for a textbook as before even though this was their second textbook and represented an increase in the quantity of books demanded.

## *Decrease in demand*

Just as consumer demand can shift right and increase at every price level, it can also shift left and decrease at every price level. The next diagram shows this scenario, following a similar format to the previous diagram as D1 is the new demand curve, with P1 and Q1 the new equilibrium price and quantity where the new demand line crosses supply line S. But here the dashed D1 line gives a possible leftward parallel shift of the old demand line, and it gives a reduced equilibrium price P1 and a reduced equilibrium quantity of sales Q1.

# Result of decrease in demand

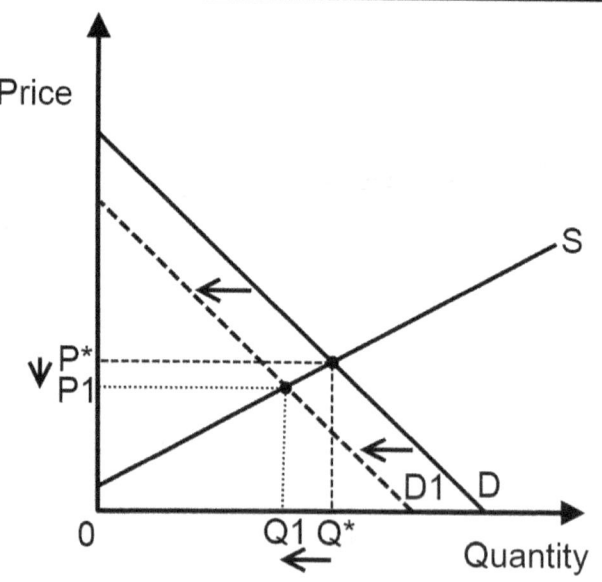

The cause of the sudden leftward shift and decrease in demand seen here would be the opposite of the causes mentioned earlier for a sudden rightward shift and increase in demand. Causes with potentially long-lasting effects which could see D shift left to D1 for a prolonged period may include consumers suddenly suffering a decreased level of income, and they have less money to spend on products, resulting in reduced demand at every possible product price. Alternately, the price of similar substitute products from rivals may have decreased, to see rivals turn away from the product here and to those substitutes instead, to reduce the demand and sales for the product depicted in the diagram. Another cause could be that the product represented here has received some bad publicity, such as a publicized link between the product and poor health, and this would reduce demand at every price and essentially operate as a very bad advertising campaign.

While the sudden leftward shift in demand and decrease at every price level may be long-lasting or permanent for a product it could also be brief and temporary. On a normal day the demand for a hot curry product, or an ice cream product, may be represented by the original demand line D, and where this crosses the supply line S determines the equilibrium, with equilibrium price P* and equilibrium quantity Q*. But on a very hot day the demand for a hot spicy curry would naturally fall at every price, as people will already be hot and many will turn to food to cool them down not hot spicy food which offers the opposite. This means demand may shift left to become the new demand line D1, which would give the new lower equilibrium price and quantity for the spicy curry at levels such as P1 and Q1 respectively, but only as long as the hot day lasts. And this exact same phenomenon would occur for an ice cream product on a very cold day, as ice cream will naturally be less popular when people are already cold, and many will turn to hot food instead.

Turning back to the textbooks example introduced earlier, if a student buys a flawless economics textbook which explains everything perfectly the student may have no further demand for any other textbooks. This would also see the demand line shift left as in the examples just mentioned, but far further left than shown in the last diagram and the line would instead shift leftwards off the entire page. This leaves no demand line for additional textbooks and the student will no longer be a consumer of textbook products, and as a result there will no longer be an equilibrium for textbooks and there will be no further transactions. This explains why textbooks may be good but never perfect, and the supplier of such a product would be working against their own interests. The creation of the perfect economics textbook would reduce the sales of the author's other textbooks if they produced a wide range, and if the author only produced one textbook it would ensure readers won't need to buy any updated editions.

## *Increase in supply*

There can also be shifts in supply in the short-run, and the principle is exactly the same as with a shift in demand. The new supply line is simply a parallel shift of the old supply line S, with the slope remaining the same but the intercept changing and being reduced. The following diagram shows the result of an increase in supply at every price level, and dashed line S1 represents the new shifted right supply line, P1 an example lower new equilibrium price and Q1 an example greater new equilibrium quantity sold, where supply crosses demand.

# Result of increase in supply

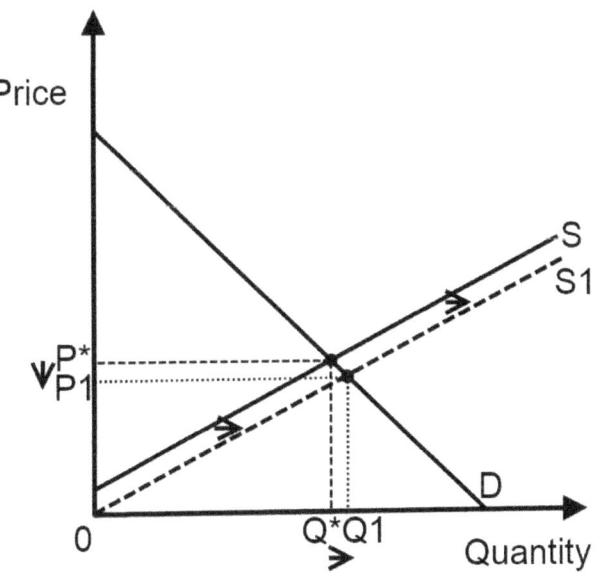

A lower price but higher supply of goods is more appealing to consumers, and just as producers or suppliers hope for sudden rightward shifts and increases in demand, consumers hope for supply increases. As with demand shifts there are various reasons why supply may increase at every price and the supply line may shift right from S to S1. The cost of resources used as inputs in the production process may have fallen, or the product supplier may have seen its competitors struggling and increased production levels to try and raise its market share. Either could result in the new supply line S1, for a lower equilibrium price P1 and higher equilibrium quantity Q1.

While the reduction in the cost of resource inputs or a strengthening of a firm's position relative to its rivals may cause a long-lasting shift right in the supply line, there are other causes of supply increases which may be temporary. For example, many firms change their product range by season and the period just before a changeover in stock, such as a change from winter wear clothes to spring wear clothes, may see a company increase its supply of stock to get rid of the old and create space for the new. Such a policy by a firm would shift their supply curve to a higher level such as S1, for a new lower equilibrium price and greater equilibrium quantity sold represented by P1 and Q1 in the diagram. But the shift will only last until the supplier finishes the stock changeover, and then the supply and equilibrium will return to the former level, line S.

## *Decrease in supply*

Just as the supply of products can increase it can also decrease to see the supply line shift left. This is shown in the following diagram, as the supply line makes a parallel shift to the left from line S to dashed line S1, to cut the demand line D at a different point. The result is an end to the former equilibrium with price P* and quantity sold Q*, which is replaced with a new equilibrium and higher equilibrium price P1, and a new lower equilibrium quantity Q1.

# Result of decrease in supply

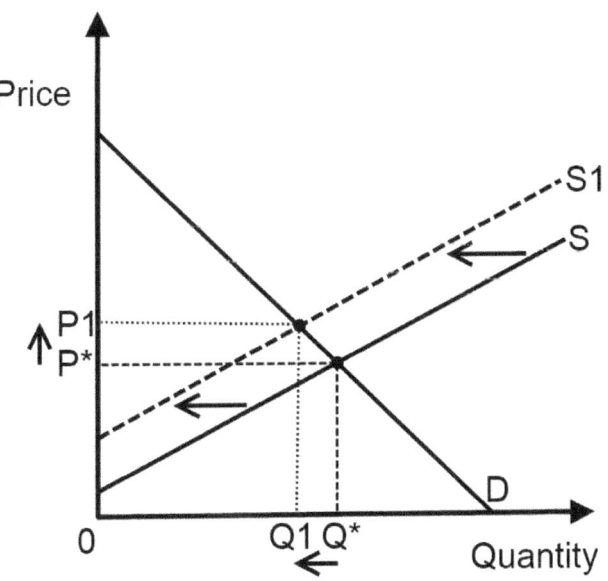

One possible cause for a sudden leftward parallel shift in the supply line, and a reduction in the quantity supplied at every price level, may be that the cost of resources used as inputs in the production process has risen. Another cause of a leftward shift in supply may be the government increasing the level of (or introducing a) unit tax on the products, and this tax would be added to the price of supply at every quantity level to shift supply up (same as shift left in supply) by that amount. Fuel or unhealthy foods are examples of products which often see sudden unit tax rises. A third explanation for reduced supply may be that a producer or supplier has seen its competitors' products outperforming their own, and it may decide to 'hunker down' and reduce its own supply to protect its market share and defend what it can, instead of leaving itself open and vulnerable. Any of these scenarios could result in a long-lasting leftwards shift of the supply line such as that from line S to line S1 in the diagram.

There is also the possibility that the decrease in supply is temporary, and that supply will shift from supply line S to line S1 and then back again. This may occur if a producer was trying out a new market or product, and it made a policy to dedicate a reduced supply of products for its trial period, to play it safe and feel out the market until it knew the product would be well received. If a product becomes established the supply line may be shifted back to line S to match the usual supply of their other products.

# The Long Run: Transformed Trends

While the short-run time factor may see curves or lines suddenly shift one way or the other, either for a long-lasting amount of time or only for a more temporary period, the long-run time factor may see curves or lines transformed completely. In the long-run the data points on which all of the prior analysis was based on can change, as the factors determining them have time to change, and consumers may demand (buy) different quantities of a good at various price levels, while producers or suppliers may supply different quantities of a good at various price levels. This naturally means that trend curves and best fit lines based on the set of data points may change, as may the equilibrium outcomes calculated from the intersection of these trend lines, and all of these may need to be calculated all over again using the methods already noted.

One of the most notable features of long-run economic analysis is that one of the assumptions put forward earlier will no longer hold. The idea of diminishing returns to production was introduced in a previous section, based on the rough idea concept that 'too many cooks spoil the broth' and that adding more workers will offer decreasing levels of return as they get in each other's way. However, this was assuming that the only production factor which could be changed was labour (i.e. number of workers, or the number of hours worked), and while in the short-run this may be true in the long-run all production factors can be changed. This means that a firm can not only change (i.e. increase) the number of workers it uses, but also the number of buildings or machinery units (known as capital) it has, and the amount of land it holds, and this brings to an end the problem of diminishing returns.

For example, a firm which hires additional chef workers won't have to put them all into one restaurant in the long-run, and it can avoid the 'too many cooks spoil the broth' problem of diminishing returns by giving them each their own restaurant (by changing the amount of buildings they use in the long-run). And the restaurant buildings won't face diminishing returns either as each can be built on a different piece of land far away from each other (as the firm can change the amount of land it has in the long-run).

Note however that the facts of diminishing returns will still hold for workers in the long-run, just as in the short-run, and if a firm only added more and more workers in the long-run without adding more buildings or land to put them in/on then it would face diminishing returns. Nothing will change this underlying economic truth. It's just that in the long-run the problem of diminishing returns to a single factor of production can be sidestepped, as additional workers can be combined with additional buildings or machinery, which can be combined with additional amounts of land, so that the effects of a single factor of production are never noticed.

Earlier diminishing returns to production (a single factor of production, labour, in the short-run) were shown using a supply curve which became steeper with greater levels of production, and this was simplified as a steep upward sloping straight line. The following diagram shows how that supply line may change in the long-run.

# A LR trend line for supply

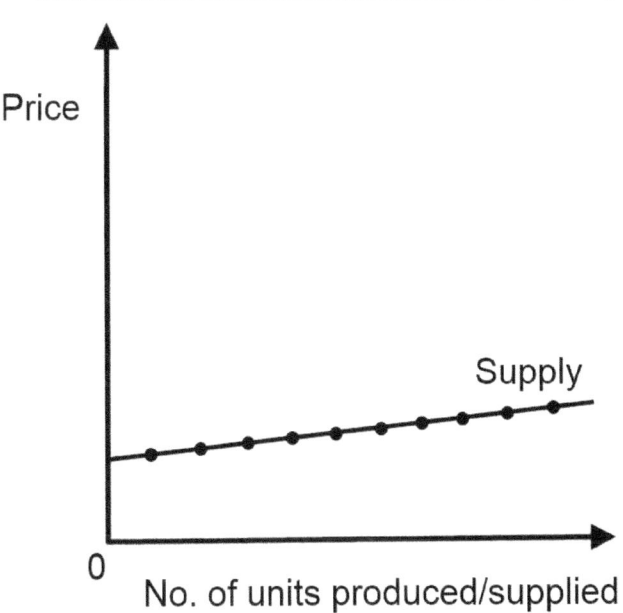

In this diagram the supply curve is far less steep than the diminishing returns curve shown earlier, and higher levels of production don't increase the level of price increase required to supply an additional unit, as shown by the data points which are positioned in a straight line shape and not in an upward sloping curve shape. The cause of this change is the elimination of diminishing returns made possible by combining different factors of production.

With only one factor, labour, adding more workers causes them to get in each other's way and reduce the increases in returns, but the cost of each additional worker will not fall in the same way (as new workers wouldn't accept a lower wage than other workers get). This was the cause of the ever steepening curve shown earlier, as higher and higher price increases were required for a firm to supply more and more products to cover the cost of increasing worker inefficiency. However, in the long-run workers are combined with new buildings or machinery or land so they don't get in each other's way, and there won't be a problem of ever larger falls in returns as production levels increase. Therefore a producer doesn't need ever higher price increases for additional units and the supply curve/line is far less steep than before, allowing high supply levels to occur at a lower price. This explains why firms which have been around a long time, and acquired more buildings, machinery, and land, can undercut newer firms without these resources with a lower price.

The supply line shown in the diagram may be flatter than before but it is still upward sloping even in the long-run, and higher levels of production are still linked with a higher price requirement by the supplier even without worker inefficiency. This is because taking on additional workers or adding more buildings for production will typically come at a greater cost, as all these things cost money, and a firm covers this cost with a higher price requirement.

It's worth noting that the long-run supply line in the diagram is only one possibility however, and in the long-run a firm may still face the steep diminishing returns supply curve shown earlier, if it only adds more workers/labour hours to boost production and ignores capital (buildings etc.) and land. And if the maximum level of supply were fixed for some reason, such as government restrictions, then in the long-run the supply curve could be completely vertical. This is because in the long-run a firm should have time and resources to reach the maximum level (creating a data point at the maximum production level on the horizontal axis), but wouldn't be able to move any higher no matter the price (creating a vertical straight line from this data point up and down, at all prices).

# Overview of Microeconomics

The previous analysis has shown how economics works, and the different steps or dimensions which economic analysis can follow. Not all of the steps will always be used, and at times there may be no need or possibility for some of them, but the different economic methods and tools can provide new insights. However, it may seem to some that almost all the analysis so far has only examined Microeconomics, and only a small part of Microeconomics at that: supply and demand. It may seem that the analysis has completely ignored other areas of Microeconomics, and ignored Macroeconomics completely, and that these other fields will need to be addressed from the beginning. But the analysis that has already been explained, with data points, curves, lines, the equilibrium, shifts in the equilibrium, and long-run transformations, has given the foundations for all of economics, and Microeconomics and Macroeconomics simply apply these to different areas.

Despite the differences between Microeconomics and Macroeconomics, the various sub-categories which make up these fields, and various applied economic topics, they have a great deal in common. And it's helpful to keep this in mind when facing new areas as it makes the process of understanding them far easier. For example, all of the prior focus and analysis has been applied to supply and demand (of a product). This could be seen as a Microeconomics topic, and it relates consumers (who determine demand) to producers (who determine supply), and relates quantity (demanded or supplied) to price:

### ***Demand and Supply***
Consumer & Producer; Price & Quantity

Other areas of Microeconomics simply look at the constituent parts of demand and supply. For example, the analysis may look at only consumers and the demand, and examine how a consumer's demand is formed.

### ***Demand***
Consumer; Price & Quantity

Consumer demand is formed by combining two areas, the price factor and the quantity factor. The quantity factor uses a series of parallel curves/lines to show a consumer's preferences. These preferences are found using economic analysis which relates one product against another, to see how many units of quantity of one product a consumer values equal to a certain quantity of units of the other product, and more of a product is assumed to be preferred to less.

## *Preferences*
### Consumer; Quantity & Quantity

And the price aspect brings prices of products into the analysis using a straight line. It relates one product against another to see the different combinations of each product which could be purchased given the consumer's income limitations, known as their budget constraint.

## *Budget Constraint*
### Consumer; Price & Price

The point where the budget constraint line crosses the (highest parallel) preference curve gives a point on a consumer's demand curve. And repeating this process again with different prices and moved budget constraints gives different points on the demand curve.

With consumers and demand for a consumer explained the next step is to look at producers and supply. As explained earlier, this relates price against supply quantity.

## ***Supply***
### Producer; Price & Quantity

The quantity of supply can be examined separately, by relating the quantity of input resources against the quantity of output resources to show productivity.

*Productivity*

Producer; Quantity & Quantity

In the short-run where labour (workers) is the only factor of production which can be changed, productivity uses the number of workers or hours worked as the inputs. Productivity may be represented with the total, average, or marginal (the change in) productivity of labour (i.e. output), and all of these will exhibit diminishing returns for reasons detailed earlier. A firm wouldn't want to operate at a production level beyond the point where the marginal product of labour is zero, as after this the total product of labour begins to decline (i.e. total output falls).

In the long-run labour (workers) and capital (buildings etc.) can both be changed, and productivity uses both as inputs. Diminishing returns to labour is no longer a problem as the firm can simply use more of the other factor of production, capital. A firm is instead concerned with returns to scale in the long-run, which shows the relationship between overall inputs and overall output. If output increases at a lower level than inputs (e.g. 2 x input levels = 1.5 x output levels) there are decreasing returns to scale. If output levels increase at the same level as inputs (e.g. 2 x inputs = 2 x outputs) there are constant returns to scale. And if output levels increase at a greater level than inputs (e.g. 2 x inputs = 3 x outputs) there are increasing returns to scale. A firm naturally wants increasing returns.

A firm's costs are also a key factor in determining its supply. Just like with productivity costs can be measured in total, average or marginal (the change) terms, and costs relate a producer's quantity of output against its cost price.

## Costs
Producer; (Cost) Price & Quantity

However, having information on both a producer or supplier's productivity and their costs isn't necessarily enough to know their supply. Common sense suggests that a firm will operate (i.e. supply output) at the point which offers the highest profit, and as profit is revenue minus costs a firm's revenue also affects the supply decision. Revenue relates quantity of output against price.

## Revenue
Producer; Price & Quantity

Revenue could be measured in total, average or marginal (change) terms. Marginal revenue is most important as this shows how revenue is changing as production increases and is the most up to date revenue measure. As the impact of the level of revenue or costs depends on the level of the other it's common to see both revenue and costs represented in the same diagram, to allow a comparison.

A firm will want to operate at a supply quantity level where two conditions are met simultaneously: 1) marginal revenue (MR) = marginal costs (MC); while 2) the change in marginal revenue is exceeded by the change in marginal costs. The logic behind this is that a firm won't want to operate at a point where MR < MC as costs exceed revenue and money will be lost. And if MR > MC then there are still more profits to be had, and a firm should push on to greater production in order to secure them. Only where MR = MC can a firm meet its costs and not miss out on future profits. Although at the production level where MR = MC there may still be additional marginal revenue to be gained if production levels were to be increased further, beyond this point MR < MC assuming condition 2 is met and the change in marginal costs will exceed the change in marginal revenue.

The MC and MR curves can vary significantly, and the type of market structure (monopoly, perfect competition etc.) can determine their shape. While an upward sloping marginal cost curve/line (marginal costs rise with production levels) and downward sloping marginal revenue curve/line (marginal revenue falls as production levels rise) may be the most common, either MC or MR may remain constant as production levels increase, for a perfectly horizontal straight line on a diagram.

# Overview of Macroeconomics

Macroeconomics builds upon Microeconomics and records the total of all demand from all consumers and all supply from all producers in a national economy, to form aggregate demand (AD) and aggregate supply (AS):

### *Aggregate Demand and Aggregate Supply*
All Consumers & All Producers; Price & Quantity

As it's based on the summation of demand and supply the basic AD-AS model is the same shape as demand and supply, with a downward sloping demand curve and upward sloping supply curve, at least in the short-run. The shape of the long-run aggregate supply curve is a matter of opinion, and followers of classical economic theory suggest it is perfectly vertical (i.e. at any price quantity is fixed at a certain point), as full employment and the associated quantity of worker supply will occur in the long-run. Other economic theorists may disagree.

AD relates to all consumers in an economy, and it compares product/service price with quantity demanded.

### *Aggregate Demand*
All Consumers; Price & Quantity

Aggregate demand is decided by the IS-LM model, which plots interest rate (price of borrowing) data against national income (quantity of national resources output):

## *IS-LM model*

All Consumers; Price (real interest rate, the nominal interest rate minus inflation) & Quantity (national income)

There are two lines in the IS-LM model. IS stands for Investment-Saving and the IS line gives all points where investment and saving are balanced, to give equilibrium in the goods and services market. The IS line shows the effect of interest rate changes on national income, and it slopes downwards as declining interest rates stimulate a move to fixed rate investments (and away from declining return variable rate investments). These fixed investments then increase national income via a multiplier effect.

LM equals Liquidity Preference-Money Supply and the LM line gives the points where the demand for money (i.e. preference for liquidity) and supply of money balance, for equilibrium in the money market. The LM line shows the effect of national income changes on interest rates, and it slopes upwards as rising national income stimulates interest rate rises. Rising national income leads to greater consumer spending and inflation, and interest rates are raised to make it more costly to borrow money and more rewarding to save it to then reduce spending and inflation.

# IS-LM model

Where the IS and LM lines cross is where the goods market and money market are balanced and in equilibrium, and this is one point on the aggregate demand (AD) line. Shifts in the LM line see a movement along the downward sloping AD curve. An increase in the money supply (by creating more money) sees the LM line shift right for a rightward move along the AD curve, while a reduction in the money supply would has the opposite effect. Shifts left or right in the IS line see the AD curve shift left or right with it, and a possible cause of a rightward shift is greater government spending, while less spending would have the opposite effect. However, the precise cause of shifts in the IS and LM lines are debated by economic theorists.

## ***Aggregate Supply***
All Producers; Price & Quantity

Aggregate supply looks at all producers and relates the price of products and services to the quantity supplied. First, there's the supply of workers, or worker hours. This uses the Phillips curve, which relates the inflation level (percentage price changes) to the level of unemployment (quantity of non-producing people) at the national level.

### *Phillips Curve*
All Producers; Price (percentage changes, i.e. inflation) & Quantity (of non-producers, i.e. national unemployment)

Economic growth models are a major area of aggregate supply. These relate the quantity of production inputs (capital and the number of workers, which may be represented by population growth) against the quantity of national income as an output. However, prolonged economic growth is thought to depend on input resources which can have increasing and not decreasing rates of return; human capital (i.e. education, worker knowledge and 'learning by doing' skills) and new technology.

### *Growth Models*
All Producers; Quantity (of production inputs) & Quantity (of national resources output, i.e. national income)

# Econometrics and Value Estimates

Previous sections have explained data points, trend curves with diminishing returns or diminishing marginal utility, best fit trend lines, the equilibrium outcome where all sides are balanced, non-equilibrium outcomes, and the changes which can occur to equilibrium outcomes, or the various microeconomic or macroeconomic fields where these may be applied. However, this has all been purely theoretical. In order to use these ideas and actually produce some tangible results which can be used to determine actions and policy numerical values need to be added to the analysis, and this is the focus of this section.

In the discussion on curves and lines earlier it was suggested that although in practice data points will tend to be curves, representing diminishing marginal utility if relating to consumption or the counterpart diminishing returns if relating to production, it is useful to see them instead as straight lines. It was explained that the advantage of this is that a straight line gives an intercept and constant slope while a curve may not have an intercept and certainly won't have a constant slope. This section builds on this and uses values for the intercept and slope.

While many people think all areas of economics either fall under a Microeconomics or Macroeconomics category there is actually a third division to the subject. This field is known as Econometrics, and it uses statistical analysis to find estimate numerical values for the trend lines and equilibrium outcomes which micro or macro theory describes.

The econometric procedure is as follows: 1) First collect a series of sample data points, which link a value of the variable under investigation (e.g. quantity of sales of a product) with the associated value of a variable considered to exhibit causation or correlation with it (e.g. price of that product when sales occurred). 2) Perform a 'regression' using statistical software (those at university or college should have access to specialist economics software, and others can use Microsoft Excel). This is done by inputting the columns of data into the software separately, with the variable under investigation chosen as the 'y variable' (e.g. quantity of sales), and the associated variable considered to be a cause or correlated with it chosen as the 'x variable' (e.g. price). The regression then calculates the estimated relationship between the two variables.

For example, if the collected data points related to consumer demand, and the number of sales at various prices, then the regression may give the estimated values:

Intercept = 17; Slope = -1.5

The following diagram revisits the demand line seen before in this book, but this time adds in these example values for the intercept where the trend line cuts the vertical axis, and for the slope. The slope shows how the variable on the vertical axis changes as the variable on the horizontal axis is increased by 1, which gives the same result as the formula given earlier where the slope = vertical axis variable change / horizontal variable change.

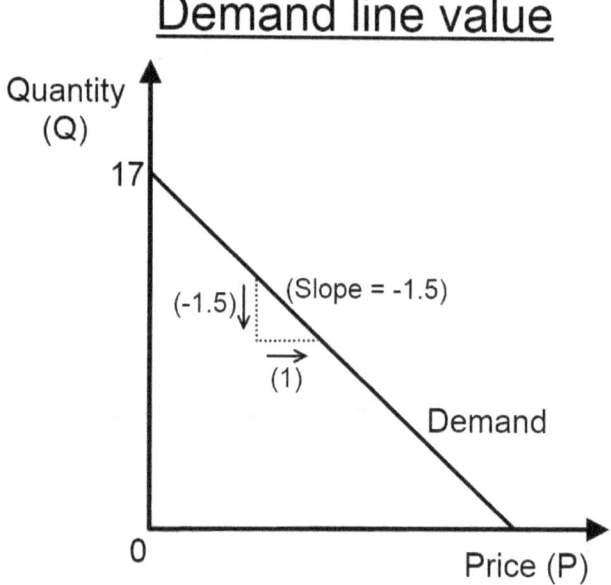

# Demand line value

One noticeable difference from the demand line seen earlier is that quantity and price have switched onto the opposite axis. This is because the earlier demand line represented correlation but econometrics uses causation, and price changes should more directly affect quantity of sales than the other way around. The change of axis shouldn't affect the analysis, but the switch of axis is essential to show quantity (Q) as a function of price (P):

Quantity demanded = quantity intercept + (slope * price)
Demand: $Q = 17 - 1.5\ P$

The same process can be applied to supply, using data on quantity of units supplied at various prices. Example estimated regression values and a diagram of them are:

Intercept = 2; Slope = 1

# Supply line values

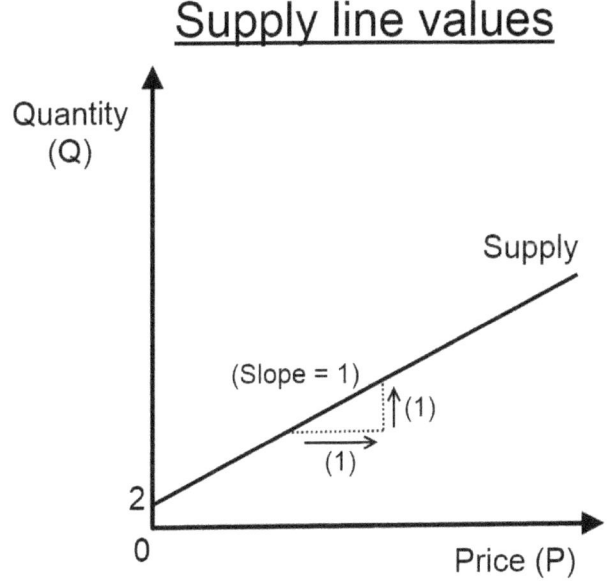

This graph shows that the quantity of products supplied is a function of price as follows:

Quantity supplied = quantity intercept + (slope * price)
Supply: $Q = 2 + P$

Estimated intercept and slope values for supply and demand lines can then be combined, as a precursor to finding example equilibrium values.

## Supply and demand values

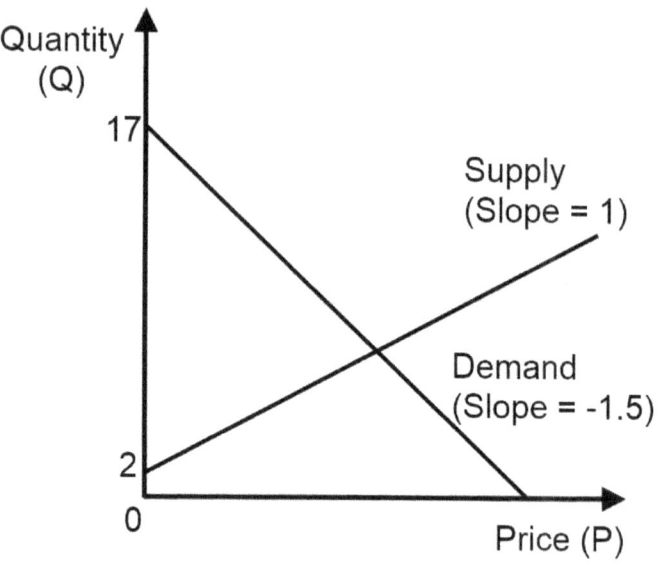

The point where the two lines cross is of course the equilibrium, as explained earlier. And this can now be calculated using the two equations for demand and supply just presented. As the equilibrium is where demand = supply the equilibrium values for price and quantity here are found by putting the two equations for demand quantity and supply quantity above equal to each other.

$$\text{Demand: } Q = 17 - 1.5\,P$$
$$\text{Supply: } Q = 2 + P$$

$$\text{Demand } Q = \text{Supply } Q$$
$$17 - 1.5\,P = 2 + P$$

First the P values need to be put onto one side only, and this can be done by adding 1.5P to both sides, which simplifies the equation as follows:

$$17 - 1.5\,P\,(+1.5P) = 2 + P\,(+1.5P)$$
$$17 = 2 + 2.5P$$

Then 2 can be subtracted from both sides to have the numbers on one side only:

$$17\,(-2) = 2 + 2.5P\,(-2)$$
$$15 = 2.5P$$

And then the value of P can be found by dividing both sides by 2.5:

$$15 / 2.5 = 2.5P / 2.5$$
$$6 = P$$
$$P = £6$$

With the equilibrium value for price found at P = £6 this value can then be put back into the equations for demand quantity and supply quantity from earlier, to find the equilibrium value for quantity (Q):

Demand: $Q = 17 - 1.5\,P$

$$Q = 17 - 1.5\,(6)$$
$$Q = 17 - 9$$
$$Q = 8$$

And this result is confirmed using the supply equation:

Supply: $Q = 2 + P$

$$Q = 2 + 6$$
$$Q = 8$$

This reveals that the equilibrium quantity (Q) is 8 units. Combining the equilibrium price and quantity together give the equilibrium outcome, where price = £6 and quantity = 8 units. This is where supply = demand, as the following diagram shows.

# Equilibrium price and quantity values

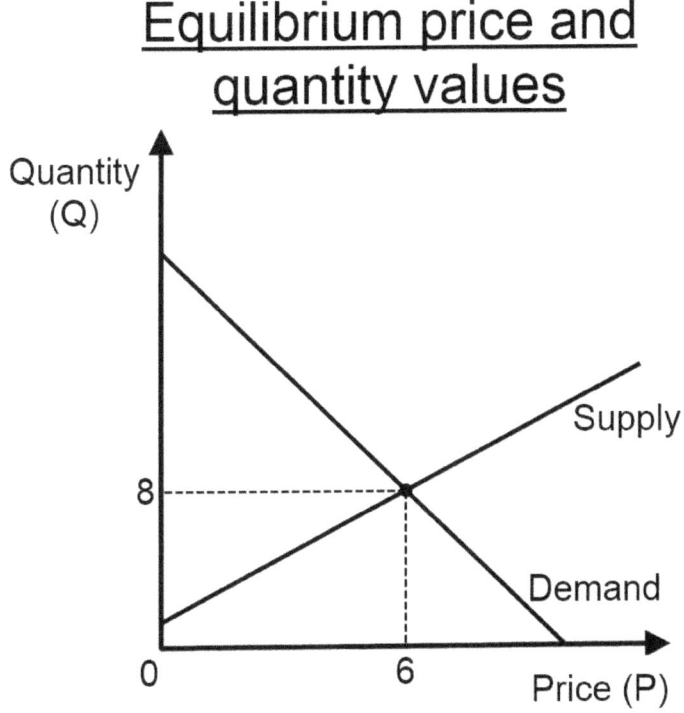

According to this result a price above £6 or a quantity supplied above 8 units will result in excess supply, while a price below £6 or a quantity supplied below 8 units will result in excess demand. Only the price of £6, quantity supplied of 8 units gives the efficient outcome.

However, the example results calculated here will not be completely accurate. Remember that the actual shape of the supply and demand trends are likely to be curves, yet are simplified as lines here to allow intercept and slope value estimates to be found, to use to calculate equilibrium value estimates. These estimates are based on the idea that demand and supply are straight lines, when they are almost certainly curves, so estimates for intercept, slope and the equilibrium will contain some error. Also, the value estimates will always be calculated from a data sample of limited size, and therefore they can only ever act as estimates and proxies for actual values in the complete data population, which will by definition remain unknown.

If there was a sudden short-run shift in either supply or demand the equilibrium values will change with them, and the estimate equilibrium values must be recalculated. This can be done using demand and supply equations but making a subtraction or addition to the constant term (intercept), based on the direction and size of the shift.

A short sample period (e.g. one year) will only represent short-run demand and supply, even if a large sample of data was used in the econometric regression (e.g. a large number and range of product prices, and associated quantity of sales). To represent long-run demand and supply and account for long-run changes in trends over time a longer-run sample time period (e.g. ten years) would be required for the econometric regression.

Finally, although the value estimates method here has been shown for supply and demand the same method can be applied to a range of areas. Applying these methods to any economic area of interest can reveal data relationships and equilibrium values.